LAW, POWER, AND THE PURSUIT OF PEACE

Other books by Eugene V. Rostow

A NATIONAL POLICY FOR THE OIL INDUSTRY

PLANNING FOR FREEDOM: THE PUBLIC LAW
OF AMERICAN CAPITALISM

THE SOVEREIGN PREROGATIVE:
THE SUPREME COURT AND THE QUEST FOR LAW

LAW, POWER,
AND THE
PURSUIT OF PEACE

BY

Eugene V. Rostow

HARPER COLOPHON BOOKS
HARPER & ROW, PUBLISHERS
NEW YORK, EVANSTON, AND LONDON

First HARPER COLOPHON edition published in 1968 by Harper & Row, Publishers, Incorporated.

The hardcover edition is published by UNIVERSITY OF NEBRASKA PRESS.

LIBRARY OF CONGRESS CATALOG CARD NUMBER: 68-25831.

To the Foreign Service of the United States,
good companions in many foxholes,
with affectionate appreciation and respect.

E. V. R.

Contents

Foreword   ix

Preface: The Problem of Peace   xiii

1. Lawful and Unlawful War: A Statement of the Issue   1

2. Order and Disorder, 1815–1945   18

3. The Truman Doctrine and World Law, 1945–1963   36

4. New Challenges to American Foreign Policy,
   1963–1968   51

5. The Major Tests, Vietnam and the Middle East   59

6. Concert and Conciliation: The Task of Building
   a New World Order   85

7. Conclusion   115

Index   127

Foreword

THIS BOOK is a revision of two Roscoe Pound lectures given at the University of Nebraska in February, 1966, under the title "The Quest for International Order and Law." They were nearly ready for publication in October, 1966, when I was called to the State Department.

I have finished the manuscript in the interstices of official time. To say that "much has happened" since the lectures were given would make even Mr. Arbuthnot blush. But I am satisfied that their argument is confirmed by the pattern of developments during the last two years.

I have of course taken recent events into account in completing this text. But I have added as little as possible to the talks I gave in Nebraska. In the course of revision, I have drawn on passages from several speeches—for some of which, in turn, I had cannibalized the manuscript of the Nebraska lectures.

The question posed in this book—the task of peace-keeping in the real world—requires us to consider how law and experience influence each other. It is hard to imagine a theme more appropriate to a lecture series in honor of Roscoe Pound. Before the monstrous totem of war, a page of history is indeed worth a volume of logic. These intricate problems, just below the edge of law's consciousness, demonstrate again that law can be studied only in its integument of reality. The premise of this essay is that international law, like other branches of law, is a product and external manifestation of social experience, which in turn it does much to shape and influence. In order to examine the development of international law, we must take into account what is generally called history, politics, public opinion, morality, and custom quite as much as the abstract sentences which purport to state legal "rules" in the law books. Such epitomes of doctrine are not the law, but a visible measure of its condition at a particular moment of time, a means of glimpsing the living process within. That proposition is a considerable part of Roscoe Pound's gospel.

There is particular satisfaction for me in having been asked to honor Roscoe Pound. As a communicant in the Yale sect of sociological jurisprudence, I am happy to acknowledge our debt to a dean of the Harvard Law School, one of the great figures in law, and, by any criterion, a high priest, perhaps even a bishop, in the cult of sociological jurisprudence.

Roscoe Pound burst upon the law school world well before my time. But he was a force among us before he became a legend, and he remained a force thereafter as well. His appointment was greeted as a progressive act, significant for all the law schools. In a *New Republic* editorial called "New Leadership in the Law," Professor Morris R. Cohen wrote, "In electing Roscoe Pound the dean of its law school, Harvard has chosen not only a man who is fit to continue the splendid tradition of Langdell and Ames, but, what is still better, one who is bound to create a new and vital tradition of his own account. . . . Mr. Pound is sure to produce [a] . . . beneficent revolution by insisting on the . . . principle that law is a social science."[1]

And so it proved to be in fact, even, ultimately, at the Harvard Law School itself. Long after others had replaced Pound as

---

[1] *The New Republic*, vol. 6 (1916), p. 148, reprinted in *Law and the Social Order* (1933), pp. 32, 37.

the mirror of fashion, he pressed upon our minds. Trained in biology, he preached the need for systematic methods in law, although he never fell into the traps of pseudo science. He knew that studying the behavior of man in society is inherently more difficult than the work of natural science, and that the example of science cannot of itself permit us to solve the characteristic problems of law—crime and sin, greed and fairness. Pound sought to make the study of law not merely a bookish, but a learned activity—far more than a way to train apprentice practitioners. Above all, he stood for a view of law as part of life, an appreciation of law as custom and history as well as theory. Despite the distractions of being a dean, he remained an active teacher and writer—an aspect of his career I find especially remarkable. Pound ranks with the academic titans of his time—with Charles Beard, for example, and John Dewey; with Arthur Corbin of our faculty; with Veblen; with Harper of Chicago, and Taussig of Harvard—all authentic members of a small, colorful, strong-minded band of outsize men who framed our intellectual universe.

I am grateful to Dean David Dow and to the faculty of the University of Nebraska College of Law for the honor of their invitation to give the lectures on which this book is based and for the warmth and interest of the visit. My colleague David Calleo helped imaginatively in the Washington phase of the venture. So also did Robert T. Grey, Jr., Reynold A. Riemer, and Alan R. Novak, with zeal and zest. The title attests my admiration for Frank Hinsley's brilliant and original book, *Power and the Pursuit of Peace*. And, as always, I am grateful to my wife, whose spirited mind and passion for the good have been as helpful and as interesting in developing the argument of these pages as they have proved to be on so many other occasions of work and life.

Washington, D.C. EUGENE V. ROSTOW
August, 1968

Preface
The Problem of Peace

THE PROBLEM OF PEACE at this juncture recalls a comment Jean Monnet made in 1949. At that turbulent and uncertain time, when Europe and China were both on the brink, M. Monnet and his collaborators were planning the European Coal and Steel Community, the first of the new European institutions. "The international situation will have to become much worse," he remarked, "before so radical a step can be taken to improve it." He was clearly right in evaluating the resistance to even the most sensible changes in custom and habit. There is doubtless the wisdom of instinct in the fact, for it assures some continuity in social arrangements. But there is risk, too, when continuity becomes somnambulism, and we carry on blindly in modes which time has made not simply obsolete but obstructive as well.

The argument of this book is that the state of the world has long since become "worse" enough, in the sense of M. Monnet's Law of Political Action, to make certain changes in our foreign policy and in the foreign policy of our allies both desirable and possible, if its great aim, the achievement of peace, is to remain within our reach.

In recent years, the United States has taken long steps in

this direction. We have explored new paths to an understanding with the Soviet Union and sought to reopen the doors behind which Communist China has immured itself. To reinforce these approaches, we have strongly supported the movement to transform the political foundations of the Atlantic Alliance and sought to achieve new thrust and new vitality in our other arrangements for regional cooperation.

But, for all men's cries and hopes, there is no détente. And the modernization of our alliances proceeds slowly. Such efforts must soon become programs of more effective cooperation if we are to avoid dangerous strains in the promising system of peace we have sought to build since 1945. Those efforts will require a confrontation with reality on the part of nations and peoples and their acceptance of collective responsibility on a new scale. They will require the continued building of habits and institutions that can—and must—become the substance of a new international public law.

All over the world, men are probing—and doubting—the premises of policy. They are tired of war, and of cold war. They assert their views and their demands with unmistakable force—sometimes in explosive demonstrations which test the fabric of society.

There is hope in this process, and risk as well. That men abominate the cruelty and madness of war, and wish it ended, attests their goodness. Their protests speak for all that is most generous and decent in us. The risk, of course, is that men mistake their wishes for reality. Nurtured by a century of isolation, our habitual view of world politics is innocent to the edge of Utopianism. We are constantly surprised that peace is not the normal state of affairs throughout the globe. With our Puritan tradition, we are inclined to blame ourselves for the world's ills. It is second nature for many of us, for example, to believe that the Cold War is our fault and would vanish if only we reduced our military budget and withdrew our forces from Europe, Asia, and the Middle East.

Such simple ideas scarcely do justice to the congested vitality

xiv

of international life—to the ambitions of vigorous leaders, the clash of national and class interests in a crowded and hungry world, the misunderstandings and hostilities among proud and bewildered cultures groping toward modernity.

Nor is an American assumption of blame for the Cold War fair to the serious and devoted men and women who direct the Communist parties of the world. We must respect their convictions and their efforts to realize the aims of their prophets. Communism is not a force of constant intensity in world affairs. But it is still a force. The interplay between nationalism and ideology is one of the crucial factors in the history of the last half century, most particularly in the process which has required the United States to become involved in world affairs. As Secretary of State Rusk has remarked, the periodic tensions in our relations with the Soviet Union have not been about polar bears in the Arctic, nor about abstract issues of political theory, but about Berlin, and Korea, and many other problems of politics and security. The month in which the Soviet Union invaded Czechoslovakia to suppress a movement toward ordinary human freedom is hardly a moment for illusion on this score.

At no time in history has effortless peace been the normal state of affairs. The rational control of force is not an accident but the product of man's noblest secular achievement, the political community organized by law.

The subject of this book is the condition of the international community viewed in this perspective, and the nature of the problem of harmony within it, in the light of the volcanic changes in its structure which have occurred since 1914. More specifically, it is an analysis of America's attempt since World War II to lay the foundations for a new system of international peace to replace the one which vanished in 1945. That effort has involved the use of force, but it has not been based on force. It has been primarily an attempt to persuade all nations and all peoples to accept certain fundamental ideas as to the nature of international society and the permissible limits of rivalry within it.

Cicero spoke of the *concordia* which defines a society—the universe of indispensable principles to which all are loyal. Without such concord on fundamentals, no society can long endure. A community, after all, is a psychological, not a physical, entity. It is not a congeries of people, places, and buildings, but an association of people who share common customs, habits, and values. Their law is a living embodiment of their creed. Every system of law worthy of the name contains another element as well, its yeast, the force indispensable to its vitality and capacity for growth: what Montesquieu called the spirit of its laws. By that phrase he meant the quintessential aspirations of a legal system for the future of the society it governs, the body of ideals which guide its evolution in response to changing ideas and changing social conditions.

At any moment of time, a legal system embodies rules of conduct reflecting the customs and values of the society as they evolve toward a goal defined by its sense of the ideal. Within the boundaries of such social rules, people organized as a society can carry on common tasks, and resolve their differences. The task of diplomacy is to convert the world community into a body politic in this sense.

The problem of international peace is philosophically the same as the problem of peaceful order within a nation. In international society, as in domestic society, order and the possibility of progress require fealty to the basic rule of all systems of law: that the nation within the international order, like the citizen within his domestic society, respect the moral obligation to obey the law. For a society of law, in which the citizen—or the nation—participates in the making of law, this is the essence of the social contract.

Beyond the metaphor of the social contract, there is a deeper reality. As human beings necessarily sharing a small and dangerous planet, we can no longer live in isolated fortresses. The threat of weapons and the promise of ideas have abolished impermeable boundaries. They require us to accept the concept of a single world society—a society hospitable to different social systems, and based on a common respect for rules of behavior which could permit each to survive, and to develop in accordance with its own preferences. We must adhere to these rules because we are by necessity members of the same society—what men used to call "the family of nations"—and therefore bound by the code it deems essential to its health and its survival.

Without concord in this sense, there can be no security, and no liberty. Until the peoples and states of the world agree to accept at least a minimal number of common norms to govern their behavior, the world is not a civilized community but a jungle.

The United Nations Charter sets forth a code which could prove to be the focal point for the development of such a system of values. But thus far its most fundamental provisions—those against aggression—have often been breached. The world today has no assurance that the basic ideas of the Charter will in fact be respected instinctively and universally. The law of the Charter has not yet become a fixed rule for international society, like the principle on which we rely for our certainty that the winner of a tennis match will be given the cup or the winner of an election the badges of his office.

The explosions of feeling and of protest in 1968 have been remarkable events—signals of dissatisfaction at a time when Western societies, at least, have never been more active in moving toward the fulfillment of their social goals. Historians may look back on 1968—as they do on 1848—as a year in which the deepest wishes of mankind were made manifest. Namier called 1848 the Revolution of the Intellectuals. It is striking that students and intellectuals have taken the lead in articulating and dramatizing the diverse dreams of mankind.

All over the world, there are visible and sometimes violent manifestations of human stress and concern over the trend of events. In most cases, these manifestations reflect the yearnings of generous and idealistic spirits. In some, they betray feelings of hostility, bitterness, frustration, and the desire for revenge. In many countries, the demonstrators seek liberty and social advance.

Occasionally, they manifest man's universal taste for violence, and his instinct of destruction for its own sake, normally but not always kept in check by the texture of his social system.

Of course, hostile forces seek to exploit those feelings, and to turn their manifestation into revolutionary channels—that is, into channels seeking a truly revolutionary transfer of power—or a situation of suicidal chaos, and not simply the acceleration of social change within the pattern of the existing order. And, of course, in the face of such threats governments have to intervene finally to restore and preserve public order. For the first time in many years, we have witnessed demonstrations precipitated by believers in bizarre doctrines of violence as an end in itself. Healthy societies invariably find ways, as they must, to encapsulate such actions, and to treat them for what they are.

But responsible men everywhere would ignore the yearnings behind these events at their peril. Time is running out. The demons of force are slipping their chains. The precarious minimum of order that has been ours since 1945 cannot last indefinitely in the present state of the world community.

If those in Western countries who protest in the name of peace conclude that certain Communist countries are in fact responsible for the absence of peace, the result could be incalculable.

LAW, POWER, AND THE PURSUIT OF PEACE

CHAPTER 1

Lawful and Unlawful War:
A Statement of the Issue

I

THOUSANDS OF PRINTED PAGES and hundreds of thousands of hours of talk have been devoted to the question whether international law is really "law."

Those who view law as no more than the command of a sovereign, to be obeyed out of fear of his policemen, regard the absence of world government as a conclusive answer to the question. International law is not law, they contend, because there is no world sovereign to enforce it. It is therefore no more than political philosophy, written down in the books of professors and other "mere" theorists, and nowhere engraved on tablets of stone.

Other ways of thinking about law are closer to the heart of things. The official efforts of enforcing agencies are not the only means for vindicating law. In large part, law is obeyed without coercion, because it corresponds to people's beliefs, and above all, because they believe in the idea of law. Custom, and the code of right behavior which prevails among a people at a given time, are far more important as a source of law than the command of a ruler. Modern legislation normally ratifies a decision a majority of the people are willing to accept, or have already implicitly

1

made. When, as sometimes happens, a statute flies in the face of habit, or even prejudice, it is not instantly obeyed merely because it has been promulgated by authority. And if a law conflicts with strongly held convictions or habits of a people, it is almost impossible to enforce, at least in a democratic society, until the law itself effects a change in mores.

In this perspective, international law is "law" quite as much as our common law, or the law European judges distill from their codes. It is enforced in the courts of every country as municipal law—that is, as part of the internal law of that country. It is drawn from custom and usage, from the decisions of courts in all countries, from treatises, and from treaties and other international agreements which are given the effect of statutes. And it is enforced, both in national courts and in the International Court of Justice at The Hague, about as uniformly and consistently as the law, say, of the income tax, or of the American Constitution: a good deal better, in many instances.

But international law has one feature for which there is no modern analogue in municipal law: the acceptance of the possibility that war may sometimes be a lawful act. Free societies allow a considerable latitude with regard to the private use of force—by way of self-defense against crimes of violence, for example; in the coercive tactics of trade unions and political parties; and in public assemblies and demonstrations intended to dramatize grievances and petition for their redress. But the tolerance of such modes of social action falls far short of the role of war in the society of nation states. The law of the system of world politics is still largely the law of "sovereign" national states whose supreme legal privilege has been—and to a considerable extent still is—the right to slaughter their neighbors in the name of the national will. In the organization of domestic societies, one can have order without law, as is the case in some of the tyrannies of history, old and new. But in the international sphere, we have often had law without order.

Mankind has resumed once more the ancient effort to make

war effectively illegal. The older international law, and the doctrines of many churches, distinguish just from unjust wars. And we are in the powerful shadow of Nuremberg, where for the first time men were condemned by a court for the crime of waging aggressive war. The Charter of the United Nations built upon these precedents when it declared illegal all wars but those of self-defense and wars waged in assisting states to defend themselves against aggression.

One should not underestimate the power of these principles because they do not yet completely control the behavior of man. No rules of law do. They already govern a considerable part of the mind and conduct of man. When, in recent years, the United States twice hesitated, and then withdrew, before bombing or invading Cuba, the acceptance of international law, and its capacity for self-enforcement, were vividly demonstrated. George W. Ball, then Under Secretary of State, successfully opposed the proposal to bomb the Soviet missile sites in Cuba. Every nation ought to act in accordance with its own traditions, he argued.[1] If the United States struck at the missile sites without warning, "we should wake up tomorrow a different country." And in Korea we had a shining example of what was, at least symbolically, collective action to enforce the rule of the Charter in the name of human society as a whole.

We know also, however, that the symbol of Korea is in part illusion, because the Soviet Union and its allies were boycotting the United Nations at the moment, so that the vote of the Security Council declaring the attack on South Korea to be aggression was not what it seemed. On the other hand, symbols are not to be dismissed as without influence in the affairs of man, so long as we do not confuse them with reality.

In large part, however, both public and official attitudes toward the United Nations do confuse myth and reality. People look to the United Nations with hope as a world government,

[1] Elie Abel, *The Missile Crisis* (Philadelphia: Lippincott, 1966), p. 64.

3

and feel it has failed because, to take one among many instances, it did not undo the Soviet suppression of the Hungarian revolution in 1956, or resolve the conflict in South Vietnam. Men generally speak of the United Nations as a separate force in world affairs, something above and beyond the nation states, rather than a place where they meet and conduct a good deal of their diplomatic business.

Confronting difficult international problems, we can never escape through the empty formula of passing responsibility to the United Nations. This mode of thought mistakes the nature of the United Nations, and its function in the world political system.

The United Nations does not exist, and is not designed to exist, save as an expression of the collective will of its members. As a method of protecting national security, the United Nations is not an alternative to our system of alliances, and our own military strength, but a means through which those alliances, and that strength, can express themselves diplomatically, and otherwise. Like any other system of law, the United Nations is not a substitute for force, but the sum of the rules through which the sanction of force can and should be used. To the extent that the law of the United Nations Charter is accepted, it can, again like other legal systems, permit the law to be enforced with minimal or token forces, and relieve most states of the necessity of being armed to the teeth, like medieval barons. But the United Nations does not displace the conception of an international balance of power which exists at any moment.

Much of our thought about world problems is plagued by this issue, which is perhaps the worst single aspect of our Wilsonian legacy. The problem is variously defined as a supposed choice between "power politics" and "idealism," between "domination of the big powers," and "equality for small nations," between American virtue and European vice. The words and ideas get almost hopelessly enmeshed. They provide one of the last arguments of the isolationists, in the form of the doctrine that we should be too proud, as we are too pure, to become entangled

4

in the dirty power politics of the world—a curious and extraordinary idea to prevail among Americans, whose domestic politics have always been human, not to say earthy, in their practical compromises and adjustments. It is an extraordinary idea in another sense as well. The course of world politics has always involved the United States in general world wars, and presumably always will. It is hard to understand how we can be expected to look after our vital national interest in controlling this phenomenon by ignoring the political events which govern it.

The United Nations is an indispensably valuable institution, but it is not and cannot soon be made a world government, nor even "a league to keep the peace," to recall the phrase generally used two generations ago to describe man's hopes for a world organization. The United Nations is not an independent power, but one means through which the prevailing balance of power can be registered and expressed. It is a forum, a place of assembly. If it were destroyed, it would have to be recreated, because it meets a vital need of international society—that is, the society of more than one hundred local and regional communities which claim the status of sovereign nation states.

President Wilson once remarked:

Not until after the Revolution of 1688 was parliament looked upon as modern Englishmen look upon it, as chiefly interesting because of the laws it could make. Not until the eighteenth century had passed its middle term did it come to be what it is now, the maker and unmaker of ministries, the maker and unmaker of governments. For at least four of the six hundred years during which it has been an instrument of constitutional government it was looked upon merely as the "grand assize," the great session, of the nation, whose function was criticism and restraint, which came together to see that the terms upon which English life was understood to rest were being scrupulously respected by the king and his advisers. . . .

We speak now always of "legislatures," of "law-making" assemblies, are very impatient of prolonged debates, and sneer

5

at parliamentary bodies which cannot get their "business" done. We join with laughing zest in Mr. Carlyle's bitter gibe at "talking shops," at parliaments which spend their days in endless discussion rather than in diligent prosecution of what they came together to "do." And yet to hold such an attitude toward representative assemblies is utterly to forget their history and their first and capital purpose. They were meant to be talking shops. The name "parliament" is no accidental indication of their function. They were meant to be grand parleys with those who were conducting the country's business: parleys concerning laws, concerning administrative acts, concerning policies and plans at home and abroad, in order that nothing which contravened the common understanding should be let pass without comment or stricture, in order that measures should be insisted on which the nation needed, and measures resisted which the nation did not need or might take harm from. Their purpose was watchful criticism, talk that should bring to light the whole intention of the government and apprise those who conducted it of the real feeling and desire of the nation; and how well they performed that function many an uneasy monarch has testified, alike by word and act.[2]

The main function Parliament served in those days, and that of the United Nations today, is to develop and express a public opinion, the ultimate source of governmental policy in a free society, and the indispensable condition of public action. The crystallization of opinion—the expression of a collective will—remains among the vital responsibilities of all parliaments, including those which possess legislative power and other powers of government. It is not a negligible public responsibility. But it should not be confused with the power to govern.

The collective security plan of the United Nations Charter rests on the experience of the nineteenth century. Reacting against the deceptions and futility of the League of Nations, it

[2] *Constitutional Government in the United States* (New York: Columbia University Press, 1908; paperback edition, 1961), pp. 10–12.

6

returns to the Congress of Vienna—the idea of a Concert of the Great Powers.

Article 24 reads, "in order to ensure prompt and effective action by the United Nations, its Members confer on the Security Council primary responsibility for the maintenance of international peace and security, and agree that in carrying out its duties under this responsibility the Security Council acts on their behalf."

The Charter recognizes that peace-keeping in the name of the United Nations is impossible, and inadmissible, without the agreement of the five world powers which are permanent members of the Security Council. If the permanent members of the Security Council do not agree, the enforcement of the Charter cannot be carried out through the forms of United Nations action. The Charter recognizes, in short, an essential aspect of the problem of peace in the political system we have inherited: that the ultimate responsibility for world peace rests with the nations of preponderant military and political power. The Great Powers may ignore local wars, revolutions, or conquests on the ground that they do not disturb the general equilibrium of power, or endanger the sense of security of the system as a whole. On the other hand, especially if one or another of the Great Powers is engaged in such activities, directly or surreptitiously, such upheavals may be deemed a threat to peace by the others, and contrary to "the general will." Reflecting the experience of a century which from Sarajevo to Saigon has often seen local conflicts escalate, the Charter of the United Nations condemns all aggression. In fact, however, the Charter has not been so literally construed.

During the Korean crisis of the early fifties, an attempt was made to modify the reliance of the Charter on Great Power responsibility in the realm of peace-keeping. Taking advantage of the self-imposed absence of Soviet and other Communist representatives from the United Nations, a resolution was passed conferring some of the responsibilities of the Security Council on the General Assembly, when the Security Council was prevented from acting by Great Power disagreement. In this respect, the amendment would have moved the United Nations back into the constitutional pattern of the League of Nations.

A protracted disagreement ensued, which lasted nearly fifteen years. Neither France nor the Soviet Union accepted the legality or propriety of the change, which fundamentally weakened the position of the permanent members of the Security Council in the United Nations, and altered one of the key ideas of the Charter. The controversy involved a submission to the International Court of Justice at The Hague, debates over assessments for the cost of United Nations forces in the Congo and elsewhere, and an attempt to deny the vote to member states which did not pay these assessments.

In 1965, the United States abandoned its effort to enforce the new rules. Implicitly, at least, we thus acknowledged that the original plan for the Charter corresponds to reality.

This, then, is the key idea of the United Nations Charter in the field of peace-keeping: that the United Nations cannot act in its own name when the Great Powers disagree. It does not follow, however, that the Charter is unenforceable under such circumstances. When the Great Powers disagree, or when one or more are associated with an aggression, the problem of peace appears in its nineteenth-century form. The rules of international law against aggression codified in the Charter can be enforced only by the political and military resistance of the other Great Powers, and of other states which rally to their view.

Thus in substance though not in form the pattern of enforcing the Charter is the same when the Great Powers agree and when they disagree. The question of war and peace depends equally and ultimately upon their will to uphold the law. In either case, they are the indispensable policemen of the Charter, whether or not the forces on police duty wear the United Nations' brassard over the sleeves of their national uniforms.

In this regard, the essential fact about our political system, like the feudal system at certain periods, is that it relies on a series of private decisions, and on private armies, to uphold the law embodying the general will. This is as true when action is taken in the name of the United Nations organization as it is when the Great Powers seek to restrain each other. In the first case, there is an air of international judgment to the decision, conferred by a vote in the Security Council or the General Assembly. But atmosphere should not conceal the underlying reality —that one or another of the key nations has decided to act in the interest of stability, and that the other nations, through a series of voluntary national decisions, have ordered their national contingents to participate in the effort. The United Nations does not have the power to "raise and maintain" armies, save on this basis.

As is the case with many other conceptions of the seventeenth and eighteenth centuries, the system of sovereign states we have inherited is sometimes thought to be self-equilibrating. It has been analogized to a solar system, or to the free market, in that natural laws of action and reaction, centrifugal and centripetal forces within the system, could be relied upon of themselves to keep order and harmony among the states. The forces for balance within the system, it was thought, were those of rational self-interest, and a natural repugnance for alien or illegitimate rule.

Faith in the automaticity of the free market died in the realm of international affairs even before it did in economics. The First World War convinced men that self-interest was not, unaided, a political force invariably capable of preventing ghastly cycles of war and conquest. The Great Depression which began in 1929 brought about a comparable transformation in men's thought about equilibrium in economic affairs. The world political system requires planning, foresight and a provision for mobilizing "contra-cyclical" influences, just as the economy does.

Thus far, the device to which men have pinned their hopes

for peace is one with long roots in historical experience—that of a balance of power to enforce the outlawry of aggressive war. What was added to this idea by the Covenant of the League and the Charter of the United Nations was machinery for continuous consultation and a high-minded and relatively independent Secretariat, a corps of international civil servants who could be relied upon to sound the alarm bells even when national statesmen slept.

By combining these two influences, it was felt, the rule of international law against aggression would be more effectively enforced. The system of nation states would have a stabilizer, an assurance of counterweight it has effectively lacked since the time of Disraeli and Salisbury, and their diplomacy of Congress. Such an awareness of responsibility on the part of the Great Powers could bring at least a minimum of order and stability to the world. It was reasonable to hope that these mediating and conciliating procedures would suffice to contain the cumulative stresses and irritations of what we like to regard as "normal" times, when the major states are reasonably content with the existing boundaries of the political system, and jars and conflicts arise only on the periphery—over issues like the nationality of Cyprus or Fiume, or the status of Goa, Suez, and Kashmir.

The need for separate and independent national action by some of the major powers to enforce the law against aggression is far greater when aggression is undertaken or sponsored by one or more of the major powers themselves. The insensate ambition of a major military power has always been the supreme challenge of the states system—the challenge of Gustavus Adolphus and Napoleon, of Wilhelm II, of Hitler, and now that of the messianic call to world revolution. If international law does not now condemn what Hitler did, it is devoid of content. But when a major power attacks the political order, the reality on which the conception of the United Nations rests is sharply revealed. The only sanction which can vindicate the rule of law, and therefore

10

the hope of peace, is the willingness of other major powers to uphold the law by the judicious and proportional use of their own force.

This stark and brutal fact is the essence of the system of world politics in which we have no choice but to live.

II

To say that force is the ultimate constituent of world politics does not imply that world politics is outside the law. Force is the ultimate constituent of domestic law too, as we have every reason to recall. The enforcement of the Fourteenth Amendment among us has recently required a good deal more than a policeman's nightstick—the movement of federal marshals and troops to Little Rock and to Oxford, Mississippi, and many other extraordinary steps as well.

Each nation uses force—domestically and internationally—in accordance with its own code, and, hopefully, in accordance also with the generally accepted rules of international law. That system of law is not a substitute for force, but a summary of the rules through which the society of nations deems it proper that the sanction of force be used to uphold the law. In the period of primarily American responsibility for peace since 1945, we have used our force prudently, cautiously, and for limited and defensive ends. We have used force in conformity with international law, in order to enforce it. When we had a monopoly of nuclear weapons, we did not seek to impose our will on the rest of the world. Nor have we even overthrown the regime of Castro in Cuba. Our use of force, by and large, has conformed to the rules, norms, and customs of our own civilization, and to the rules of the Charter of the United Nations. But we have used power nonetheless, because power is the final constituent of social organization. In one perspective, indeed, the main preoccupation of law—domestic and international alike—is to control the exercise of power in ways which fulfill accepted social and ethical purposes.

11

The uses of power are governed in each case by the whole content of the culture in which men assert their authority. However much the exercise of power is circumscribed by history, courts, elections, charters, constitutions, or other mechanisms of control, there is no evading the fact that it is power we are talking about, and power which has the last word. Nothing can alter the fact that there are large and small states, states with and without military power. Power is exercised differently by different countries, according to their cultural habits, just as the ultimate police power within a state is differently used in Switzerland, say, and Roumania, in Haiti and in Vermont. Canada, the small neighbor of a great power, faces different military risks than Korea. The imaginary alternative between power and another foundation for political life is false, and the prevalence of the idea conceals and confuses real issues.

Yet the idea has a persistent appeal. A characteristic statement of the late Prime Minister Nehru, and some of the declarations made before the Assembly of the United Nations on events in Hungary during 1956, betray the weakness of this view. The Prime Minister said, "As we stand today . . . all these pacts and alliances are completely out of place. . . . They are unnecessary. We have developed a very strong protection (world public opinion) against a country which acts wrongly. Why not adopt this protection instead of these armies and armaments and so on?"[3]

Prime Minister Nehru changed his views on the role of force in the international order during the last years of his life, when China threatened India on its northern frontiers.

In the two decades since the end of the Second World War, such order as we have known has been achieved and maintained by the threat or the fact of forceful Western resistance to relatively cautious Soviet or Chinese experiments in limited aggression. We have seen a series of moves and countermoves—probes by one or another of the Communist states, and measured

[3] Address at United Nations Reception, December 20, 1956, *The New York Times*, December 21, 1956, p. 4, cols. 6–8.

Western responses, leading ultimately, at least thus far, to stand-still if not to stalemate. We normally regard the Truman Doctrine, in which the principle of this resistance was articulated, as a rule of politics, and of a most primitive kind of politics. It is also, however, a rule of law, identical in substance with the principles which were deemed applicable to the United Nations' action in Korea.

The various attempts in this cycle have taken a wide variety of forms, from general strikes in Italy and France to threats against Turkey and Iran, the blockade of Berlin and the civil war in Greece, and the attacks on South Korea and South Vietnam. Sometimes, as in Europe, Western countermoves have involved a considerable array of allies, including both large and small powers. And in the attempt to conquer South Korea, which occurred while Britain and France were still actively involved in the Far East, the forces resisting aggression were international in character, although the bulk of military assistance to the Republic of Korea was American.

People sometimes ask whether the United States is or should be the world's gendarme, and whether we are acting arrogantly, and improperly, in taking so much of the responsibility for action to resist aggression, especially in Laos and South Vietnam. The question answers itself, if it is examined in the light of the Charter of the United Nations.

That document rests on the premise that there are five major world powers, which are entitled to permanent membership in the Security Council because in the nature of things they have permanent Great Power responsibility for the enforcement of the Charter and the maintenance of peace.

Time has transformed this premise, which now seems little more than a precatory fiction. Since the war, two of the five—the Soviet Union and the United States—have been super-powers. Two others, Britain and France, are medium-sized nations, much buffeted by the strains of the war and of decolonization, and now largely absorbed in the political and economic task of reorganizing Europe. They have been gradually withdrawing from active participation in the political life of Asia. As for China, the fifth permanent member of the Security Council, the world has thus far failed to solve the problems involved in the recognition of the Communist regime in China, and its admission to the United Nations. Thus, at best, the five are four, and often fewer, especially when questions of peace in the Pacific are raised.

As we have seen, the Charter is not suspended if one of the permanent members of the Security Council engages in aggression, or sponsors it. The procedures of the Security Council are not then available, but the interests and obligations of the remaining Great Powers are exactly what they would have been if the Security Council had acted to condemn the aggression. Since the withdrawal of France from Indochina in 1955, and the diminution of British interest in Southeast Asia, the United States has been in fact the only permanent member of the Security Council in a position to withstand aggression condoned by the Soviet Union or Communist China, and to rally a group of smaller regional powers willing to share in this effort.

The reason why the United States is still largely responsible for peace-keeping in Asia becomes self-evident if we examine the 1945 premise of Great Power responsibility in the light of the realities of 1968. China is still outside the equation; Europe has not yet become a political entity; Britain and France are abstaining for the time being; Japan and Germany have not yet returned to positions of full participation in world politics.

It follows, therefore, that when North Vietnam probes the dikes of order, with the tacit or overt support of China and the Soviet Union, only the United States can resist, until, as in the case of Korea, China and the Soviet Union or both come to join us in the judgment that the game is too dangerous to be tolerated.

There is nothing novel, at least since 1945, in American responsibility as the world's leading policeman. Our position in Vietnam is no different in fact from that we took in Greece,

Berlin, or Korea, although the centrality of American responsibility is perhaps more evident in Vietnam than it was in the earlier crises of the Cold War. In many of those crises, our European allies made great exertions in behalf of peace. But the disposition of forces in the postwar period was such that European resistance to a Soviet threat would have been unthinkable without full American backing. When the Soviet Union or China is involved in aggression, or approves it, American willingness to resist is the only relevant fact, and the indispensable one, if the fragile peace of the Cold War is to be preserved. In such cases, we are the world's policeman, for without our will, and our force, there could be no resistance.

This conclusion does not imply that the United States is the world's chief policeman on a universal basis. Many episodes of world politics raise questions of turbulence without involving the Soviet Union or China, or otherwise threatening the general equilibrium. In some instances, the United States and the Soviet Union agree on how the threat to peace can be resolved, or dealt with diplomatically. In others, they may disagree, but one defers to the other, because the episode has taken place in an area of special concern to its security, or because it is not deemed inherently important enough for a major showdown.

The international law of the system of world politics is not yet in fact the Utopian order evoked in some interpretations of the United Nations Charter. Those doctrines, like the precedent of Nuremberg, are new shoots in an old forest. The international law-in-fact—the living international law of day-to-day practice—is quite different. Its conventional formulations are still largely derived from the experience of the nineteenth century, and of earlier centuries. But that law was addressed to the conditions of an altogether different world community. It therefore fits the political conditions of our times most imperfectly: often, indeed, not at all. The older international law could hardly have classified phenomena of the Cold War we take for granted as compatible with "peace"—partial boycotts, for example, or the support of guerrilla armies which invade neighboring states. On the issues which are the subject matter of this book—the problem of war in our world, and whether it can be controlled—contemporary international law corresponds neither to the law of the past, nor to that of our aspirations for the future.

My effort here will be to consider the law of war and peace in relation to the political system as it is, and the process through which it is evolving. The ambitions of the Charter of the United Nations are among the forces influencing that evolution. As yet, however, they are by no means the dominant factor in the process. One of the problems I should like to examine is that of defining the political conditions that have to be met before we can achieve a state of order in the world community, and a quality of concord in its atmosphere, which might permit the dream of the Charter to become the law in fact.

I shall approach the task in the perspective of American foreign policy, for a number of reasons. In the first place, it is difficult for an American to do anything else.

But there is a justification beyond psychological necessity for this perspective.

A generation ago, in his famous *Trahison des Clercs*, Julien Benda accused many of his fellow intellectuals of betraying their most sacred obligation. Intellectuals, he reminded them, are members of a privileged estate. By tradition going back to medieval times and beyond, they belong to a universal brotherhood of learning, and of learned men. The canon of that brotherhood imposes high obligations on its members: rigor in the use of reason, courage in proclaiming unpopular conclusions, and above all loyalty to human values which transcend the special interests of class or nation.

So far as the problem of peace is concerned, there has been no basic conflict in recent years between our national citizenship and our citizenship in the human race. For twenty years, the foreign policy of the United States has been the main bulwark of peace in the world. The idea we call the Truman Doctrine—

16

the policy of containing aggression, in order to make peaceful coexistence possible—has been the only alternative to chaos in world politics, the only factor standing between us and the near-certainty of general war. The national interest of the United States is to achieve and preserve an equilibrium of forces, and a state of opinion, which could sustain peace. This is also the general interest.

It is not easy to be sanguine about the possibility of relative success in this effort, given the nature of man, and of world society. All the factors usually considered to represent "rational self-interest" favor peace. But they always do. Despite our experience with the release of hatred and aggression during the last half century—or perhaps because of it—we are loath to give the Devil his due. The forces of evil are immensely strong, and the habit of war is immensely deep in the psychic expectations of man. Perhaps Nobel's dream will come true at last—that modern weapons make war so horrible that it will vanish. Montaigne thought gunpowder would accomplish the same miracle. We must, however, continue to live by the motto of William of Orange, "It is not necessary to hope in order to begin, nor to succeed in order to persevere."

Since war, large or small, is a function of disequilibrium in the world's political system, I propose to start this analysis with the problem of order, which is one of the two perennial issues of law: the other, of course, is justice. One could begin anywhere in the tangled history of war. For present purposes, it seems helpful to start with the Congress of Vienna in 1815, the beginning of the modern world.

CHAPTER 2

———— • ————

Order and Disorder, 1815–1945

THE SOCIETY OF NATIONS has had to confront the problem of its basic structure at several critical moments in modern history. The first half of the seventeenth century, like the first half of this one, was a time of limitless and terrible warfare. Throughout most of the eighteenth century, on the other hand, Europe existed in relative tranquillity within the system of order established by the Treaty of Westphalia in 1648. That system finally disintegrated in the tumult of the French Revolution.

The era that preceded our own began with the attempt at the Congress of Vienna in 1815 to bring international violence under international control. The first task of that Congress was to tame the energies set loose in the world by the French Revolution.

The French Revolution is a power in the memory of Western civilization—perhaps of all modern civilization. We cannot know whether the extraordinary place of the Revolution in our minds is due to the shock of the events, or to the quality of the literature and art which have kept the story alive. What we do know is that generation after generation finds parables in the experience of Robespierre and Marat, of Napoleon, of Fouché, and even of Louis XVIII. Like the Paris revolutionaries of 1871, Lenin and his colleagues saw themselves as Jacobins in the costumes of Thermidor, or, imitating the imitators, as Communards. The Cultural Revolution of Mao Tse-tung invoked the Paris Commune as its ideal in 1966. The modern imagination is still preoccupied with these events, strange and terrible, but all too credible to us as well, shot through with appeals both to our nightmares and to our aspirations. Writers turn to the Revolution almost as often as to the classical myths, and for the same reasons.

Compared with some of its modern successors, the French Revolution had the good fortune to be put down. At the time, idealists protested that a reactionary coalition, the Holy Alliance of the Old Regime, was snuffing out the most generous hopes of mankind. The course of events belied their fear. "Liberty, Equality, and Fraternity" were not defeated at Waterloo, nor banished at Vienna. The cynical manipulators of Vienna earned the gratitude of mankind—a reward, be it said, they have never received. No statues or boulevards commemorate Talleyrand, Metternich, and Castlereagh. Alexander I has had better luck as a legend, but his blueprint for a federated Europe was soon given up for the more cautious plans of Metternich and Castlereagh. Metternich and Castlereagh are not folk heroes and figures of myth, like Danton. When they are remembered at all, they are dismissed as men to mistrust, trimmers and "operators," not to be compared with the *exaltés* of the Revolution, who still excite romantic minds. But they served the cause of man incomparably well. They helped rescue the Revolution from its own insanities and those it released: the terror and the guillotine; the lists and the tumbrils; the Committee of Public Safety; and the response they finally evoked, the dictatorships of the Consulate and of Napoleon. France and Europe were returned to less feverish patterns of politics.

Within more stable systems of national and international law, the Revolution after 1815 became a moral and intellectual force, which quickly transformed the politics of the world beyond all recognition. The *Ancien Régime* was never in fact restored. The nineteenth century did not turn out to be a repetition of the eighteenth. But the promise and the threat of the Revolution have been abundantly fulfilled. Its promise is the benevolent continuing history of democracy and social progress, and the spread of nationalism in Europe, in South America, and finally in Asia and Africa. Its threat is equally visible: it too is drawn from the same twin ideas of democracy and nationalism.

The Revolution advanced as equally self-evident the claim of liberty for the individual and of autonomy for the nation. Both men and peoples, our Declaration of Independence proclaimed, had a natural right to freedom. But the claim of a "people" to govern itself through a state based on its language, its customs, and its territory has not always been a benign force. It has often resulted in such turbulence and disorder as to threaten individual liberty. The peoples and languages of Europe are too thoroughly mixed up by history to match the simple principle of the national state. Nor is Europe alone in this respect. The tensions implicit in the principle of national self-determination are not unknown in Canada, and they are endemic in Africa and Asia.

During the nineteenth century, the idea transformed Europe. Everywhere one turned there were resentful minorities, and neighbors eager to annex border provinces in the name of natural right. Over and over again, the dream of liberty for the nation proved the undoing both of social peace and of liberty for the individual. It washed away empires centuries old, and made the idea of nationality supreme in the hierarchy of man's loyalties.

The elevation of the Folk and its spirit to a position of primacy released other forces in social life, often dark ones. All modern societies have witnessed the shadow or the reality of the ancient phenomenon Ortega y Gasset called the Revolt of the Masses—recurring outbursts of hatred and barbarism, seeking to destroy civilization in the name of justice. On occasion, new despotisms have seized power in the course of such upheavals, usually in the chaotic aftermath of war; sometimes they have succeeded in holding it. And the chance of peace has suffered under the impact of nationalism carried to self-defeating ends—in the multiplication of small states, and the occasional degeneration of nationalism into xenophobia.

Whether on balance the French Revolution was a "good thing," taking into account the achievements and the tragedies to which it led, is not a serious question, as Sir Denis Brogan has pointed out. The event occurred, whether inevitably or by chance, giving rise to wars and reforms, progress and reaction, the formation of modern Germany and Italy, and above all to the propagation all over the world of a magic faith that someday the Revolution would come, a day of judgment and deliverance, when, as Sir Denis remarked, "the bastilles would be stormed and the evil past buried."

Reflection might have suggested to the Paris workers, and to the proletariat that was slowly growing up elsewhere as France reluctantly began to adjust herself to the industrial revolution, that the pursuit of happiness by revolutionary methods was a mug's game, that the chance of a country so overwhelmingly bourgeois (counting the peasant proprietors as bourgeois as, economically, they were) accepting the dictatorship of the proletariat was slight and the powers of repression very formidable.

But reflection was not and is not the *forte* of the French working man. For he has the revolutionary tradition in his blood, he has inherited the unshakable belief that there *is*, that there *must* be a revolution which will not be a swindle, that the century and a half of pursuing liberation by root and branch violence *cannot* have been a blind alley, that the hopes of '93 are still valid. So it is not only unnecessary but wrong to make an accurate estimate of the forces at work in France and the world. "Revolution" was the blessed word, Mesopotamia, that gave comfort and stilled doubts. Jacobinism, now transformed into Bolshevism, was and is the opium of the French proletariat. So the Communists split the unions and split the Socialist party, moved from one extreme of policy to another at outside dictation and failed even to attempt to exploit the collapse

21

of 1940 (to which they had, of course, notably contributed). When the Prussians entered Paris in 1871, the reaction was the Commune. When the Nazis entered Paris in 1940, when the regime was as discredited as the Empire had been in 1870, the reaction was to ask permission to resume publication of *L'Humanité*, suppressed by Daladier. It was Pétain, not Hitler who objected. Such was the result of turning the revolutionary tradition over to an outside firm.[1]

The settlement after Waterloo sought to destroy every trace of the Revolution. But the reactionary spirit of the early nineteenth century, strong though it was in faith, did not dare in fact to use the ruthless methods of the Revolution. The result, by and large, was a stodgy, cautious, and repressive world, but not one of full-blown tyranny. Europe evolved into a constellation first of traditional, and later of national states, more or less guided by a Concert of the Great Powers. The main ideas of the Revolution, nationalism and democracy, revealed their potency, often in conflict. But they were kept under tolerable control. The system of international order established at Vienna functioned remarkably well until the nineties, and a Bismarck or a Churchill could probably have saved it before 1914. There were revolutions and uprisings, and limited wars. But there was no general war.

The states system of the nineteenth century is hardly a model to which we can turn with enthusiasm. In temperament and outlook most Americans, including the present author, would surely have been among the rebels of 1848 and other explosive moments of its history. But the system functioned better than any we have had for the governance of international politics since the heyday of the Roman Empire—a great deal better than the states system of the twentieth century. Except for a few enclaves like Ethiopia and Tibet, the whole world was brought into a single magnetic field. And that field was organized by accepted

[1] *The Price of Revolution* (London: 1951), p. 14.

22

law as a system of order, in which international war played a smaller part than had been the case for many centuries.

The order which derived from the settlements of 1815 was not everywhere a notably just order. It violated many of the most cherished precepts of the French and American revolutions. In many regions of Europe, it fostered the atmosphere Stendhal etched with dazzling acuity in *The Charterhouse of Parma*. It tolerated human slavery, and in large part it was based on imperial rule—often harsh imperial rule—over subject populations.

But in the perspective of our theme here—the problem of war—let us give the statesmen of the nineteenth century their due. From the point of view of the greatest good of the greatest number, there is a case to be made for the system they conducted.

In the first place, it was—most consciously—a system. Brought to the edge of disaster by Napoleon, the leading powers of Europe accepted a common responsibility for maintaining general conditions of external peace in a society whose culture they were conscious of sharing. The ambitions of each state were modulated. Each tempered its aspirations in the interest of general equilibrium. None would seek hegemony, in the model of Napoleon, until the time of William II.

The key to the Congress settlement is that the governments who made it, who were all reeling under the impact of Napoleon, were obsessed by the need for a balance in the earlier sense but revolted by the thought of returning to balance of power politics as between themselves. The Congress system was essentially the first attempt in history—as its almost exact repetition in the shape of the United Nations' experiment has so far been the last—consciously to find an alternative both to the old aim of domination by one Power, of which the latest practitioner had just been laid low, and to the balance of power as it had operated in the eighteenth century, from which all felt it imperative to escape. If, as Sorel wrote, a coalition of states founded on public law for the defense of that law would

23

have been an historical paradox in the eighteenth century, unattainable if not unthinkable, this is precisely what the Congress system was and what all statesmen agreed to be the essential solution to both these dangers.[2]

Secondly, their system was universal. Under it, the world constituted a single economy and in many respects a single society as well. Men traveled without passports, save to Russia. In ever increasing numbers, as they had for centuries, students from many countries came to the great universities of Europe. When European artisans finished their apprenticeships, they normally spent a few years traveling and working all over Europe and America. Capital, labor, and the essential skills flowed to every part of the world with unexampled freedom. Waves of immigrants journeyed to the new countries of North and South America, Australia, and South Africa. The non-European cultures began to go through intricate processes of response to the many stimuli of European civilization, the most powerful influence to which they had ever been exposed. The results were dynamic in all cases; in many, explosive; and in some, catastrophic.

Different non-European societies reacted differently, depending upon their own histories, and the form of their contact with the West.

The ordered hierarchic society of Japan mastered the secrets of European knowledge and technique without losing political control of the nation, and without a formal revolution. The experience of Japan in this regard defines one end of the spectrum. It is by any criterion the most successful adaptation of European methods to the ways of a non-European society. With its intricate cross-relationships between the European and Asian elements in the social process, the modernization of Japan is the most instructive of all the case histories of what is popularly called "development" or "modernization" in non-European countries, and an absorbing and important sociological event in itself.

[2] F. H. Hinsley, *Power and the Pursuit of Peace* (Cambridge: Cambridge University Press, 1963), p. 196.

Africa represents the other end of the spectrum, with the horrors of the slave trade and then the varieties of more-or-less-primitive colonialism in its several European settlements. Almost everywhere in Africa, older civilizations disintegrated or were destroyed in brutal contact with the new. Processes of modernization have recently begun, in a number of forms. They face formidable obstacles. The inheritance of history will burden African life for a long time.

One can classify the impact of Europe on most of the other non-European societies somewhere between these two extremes.

India acquired much that is needed for modernization from its relationship with the British—in education, law, administration, and language. It has the advantage of established nuclei of modern commerce and industry, as well as a government in the contemporary sense, capable of undertaking the tasks a modern society requires of its governments. But the combination of indigenous and European factors in the social process of India has not yet proved to be so efficient as that in Japan. And the auguries for India's future are still uncertain.

China, on the other hand, came to accept the idea of modernity late, and, as John Fairbank points out, resentfully.[3] Under the control of its Communist Party, it is now attempting to achieve a mastery of the European magic it long disdained.

Similarly, one can remark particular patterns for like transformation in Indonesia and Egypt, Malaysia, Burma, and the Philippines. For present purposes, however, we need simply note the phenomenon itself, and not the diversity of forms it has taken.

During the nineteenth century, people, goods, and knowledge flowed from Europe to the entire world on a gigantic scale, and at an accelerating pace. Education, technique, finance, and trade touched every country, and started powerful currents of change.

[3] See John Fairbank, "The People's Middle Kingdom," *Foreign Affairs*, vol. 44, no. 4, July, 1966.

These transforming processes took place within a world political system of overall stability. A balance of power was achieved, and preserved. The achievement was not easy, nor was it painless. There were limited wars, and a good deal of jostling, political and military. In no country was foreign policy conducted consistently, and according to clear plans. There was confusion about ends, and about means as well. But somehow, for nearly a century, following the tutelage of the men of Vienna, the leading nations of Europe managed to live together, and to conduct the affairs of most of the globe, without falling into a general war.

Their achievement took decisive form in the anxious struggle with the ghost of Napoleon. The experience of the French Revolution, and of a conqueror who nearly achieved complete hegemony, shocked the statesmen of the time into a determined and sustained course of diplomatic action. Under new circumstances, they sought an equilibrium. Their minds were organized by ideas about peace which had begun to take shape after the settlement of 1648, and had then developed, step by step, during the eighteenth century.

The debate about the conditions of peace involved statesmen and writers, and the opinions of parliaments and their constituencies as well. There were universalists, like Cobden, Bentham, and the elder Mill, who, reviving the dream of Dante, saw no hope of abolishing war save through a universal government, a new Roman Empire. The strong British and American peace movements favored reaching this end by persuasion and agreement. So did most of the nineteenth-century advocates of organizing Europe as "a confederal society," although some, favoring social revolution as well as peace, did not always resist the appeal of union achieved by the missionary power of a prophet, his gospel, and perhaps his sword as well. Others, following Rousseau and Kant, distrusted large states, and their moments of pride and arrogance. They thought the chances for peace were best in an international order of smallish states of approximately equal size, restrained and disciplined in their dealings with each other by mutual respect, mutual fear, and a sense of community. In such a political system, they thought, war could be confined, perhaps outlawed. It could never be total war, so long as each state accepted the right of the others to continued existence and to internal autonomy. One could quarrel about Alsace, but not about the survival of France.

The evolution of thought about peace did not occur in an intellectual vacuum. It took place against the background of events which had their own impact on the societies of Europe and the world and on the governments those societies created. The revolution of science revolutionized technology, economic processes, and trade. A new middle class emerged, that of the industrial entrepreneurs, bolder and more venturesome than the older bourgeoisie of merchants and their bankers. The productivity of land increased, allowing men to work in factories and to live in cities. Central governments, performing new functions, became more and more important, gradually eclipsing the influence of older local and regional authorities. With easier communication, more education, more internal migration, and more democracy, the advanced societies became more unified and coherent. Their sense of nationhood was intensified and their sense of social justice changed. Furthermore, international movements of goods, money, and people became increasingly vital aspects of life in the developed communities. They reinforced the tendencies which in such communities led to the emergence of the modern state.[4]

Thus, when the men of 1815 resumed the effort of their predecessors to achieve peace through diplomacy, they did so in a world which had a certain shape, and certain memories. Czar Alexander had visions his colleagues thought wildly dangerous—a universal government in Europe based on Christian principles, and achieved by enthusiasm rather than conquest. For Metternich and Castlereagh, Alexander's plans were almost as threatening as

[4] F. H. Hinsley, *Sovereignty* (London: C. A. Watts, 1966), chap. 6.

those of the emperor who had just been defeated with so much difficulty.

Metternich had to preserve the multinational Austrian Empire against the insidious idea of revolutionary nationalism. He did so with infinite finesse by balancing France against Russia, sustained by Britain's intermittent help, and that of his ultimate nemesis, the Prussia of Stein. For Metternich, diplomacy had to protect the peace not only against aggression, but against a recurrence of revolution, either in France or elsewhere. He therefore favored not a general government for Europe, but a willingness on the part of the Great Powers to take collective action in behalf of order, and against the threat of revolution, even when no serious external aggression was involved.

Castlereagh faced a different restraint, that of public opinion in a liberal democracy, where a considerable body of thought shared the enthusiasm of the revolutionaries. The generous zeal of Wordsworth, Byron, and Shelley represented a vital reality in British public life. Castlereagh's policy was therefore more limited than Metternich's: to preserve a prudent balance of power, respecting the independence of states and avoiding interference in their internal affairs, even if revolution broke out, except where such turbulence might threaten the general peace. He was more interested in equilibrium than in legitimacy, save for disturbance emanating from France, or involving a recrudescence of its revolutionary *élan*. He remained sensitive to such risks, although he suspected many of Metternich's reports of insurrections directed by a malevolent Committee of Revolution sitting secretly in Paris.

Thus was born the Quadruple Alliance, which represented an ambiguous mixture of the concept of international relations of an island power and of the knowledge of the elements of stability of a statesman with a European vision.

As in all of its relations with the revolution, Britain was confronted by a conflict of its desires with its domestic legitimization, of the wish to preserve the Bourbons with the prin-

ciple of non-interference in the domestic concerns of other
states. The result was a compromise which guaranteed Europe
against French aggression, while evading a definite commitment of common action against domestic upheavals. Its avowed
aim was the protection of the territorial arrangements of the
Second Treaty of Paris and this was undoubtedly the aspect
which appealed most strongly to the British Cabinet. Since
the territorial balance had been repeatedly disturbed by Napoleon, an exception to the principle of non-interference was
made in his case in the second article of the Alliance which
provided for the exclusion of the Bonaparte family from the
throne of France. But what if France should undergo a revolution other than Bonapartist? To make the fact of a revolution
a cause of war was to give up the principle of non-interference.
But to remain aloof might lead to another series of revolutionary contests. This dilemma was solved by an evasion by which
the insular power admitted that European stability had a social
component, while hedging its commitment in deference to
public opinion: the Allies agreed to remain "watchful" in case
"revolutions should again convulse France . . . and to take
the measures necessary for the safety of their respective states."
Revolution in France was thus declared a potential threat, even
if it did not engage in any act of physical aggression, but it
was not automatically a cause of war.[5]

The compromise policy on which the allies agreed included
procedures of diplomacy which were as important to the peace
as the idea of equilibrium itself. For Castlereagh realized that
something more than the old diplomacy was required to preserve
the unity of the Alliance, and the moderation and sagacity he
hoped would represent its concerted influence. A policy of moderation and balance, he knew, could be sustained only if the
allies remained in continuous consultation. The nature of the
modern states system, resting on the premise of nearly anarchic
prerogative, hardly permitted the Alliance to become a European

[5] Henry A. Kissinger, A World Restored (Boston: Houghton
Mifflin, 1957), pp. 185–186.

government, as the Czar proposed. The idea of the state was too strong for that, and too strong as well to allow each to give the others a veto over its policy. But they could and in effect did agree to consult each other before acting. That is a great deal.

In the context of the time, the psychological forces making for their agreement were strong. The memory of the revolutionary era was still raw. And the allies were conscious of their shared interests, their fellowship in a common civilization, and their interdependence in a threatening world. None of the governments which had combined to put down Napoleon was possessed of his demonic ambition; for nearly a century, Europe was to be spared the specter of a new conqueror. Under the circumstances, the practice of regular consultation was enough to produce a measure of concert, and, where concerted action was not achieved, of understanding. Mutual suspicions were minimized. And a pattern of politics was achieved in which the Great Powers were acknowledged to be responsible for the general conditions of peace. Their trusteeship somewhat mitigated the theoretical anarchy of the universe of sovereign states. A balance of power of considerable stability was achieved and preserved.

Something more was achieved as well. The French Revolution threatened the internal life of every society, much as the Communist movements did after both world wars, by calling for uprisings, and helping to bring them about. We had a taste of the effort in the United States, in the mission of Citizen Genêt, which led even Jefferson to protest. The machinations of the Paris Committee alarmed men in the early nineteenth century quite as much as those of the Third International, the Comintern, and the Cominform did a century later. Responding to the threats of this pressure, the nineteenth-century balance of power was still one of limited and dispersed authority. It rested on political premises which were reflected in an accepted international law. Save where the Great Powers perceived threats to the general order, and the general will for peace, it was a law which developed and, on the whole, lived by the principle of nonintervention in the internal affairs of states. War was not outlawed. But it was limited. It never became total war. The Crimean War and the Franco-Prussian War were typical of the nineteenth century in this respect. They were typical also in the anxious debates to which they gave rise about which country was the aggressor, an issue of novel importance to the statesmen and people of the age. Each state accepted the continued existence of the others, and their right to internal autonomy, except in the sacred name of the self-determination of peoples.

The principle that every "people" had a natural right to form a nation, and a national state, emerged slowly from the French Revolution. In the end, it destroyed the possibility of equilibrium. Italy and Germany were formed, and the Austro-Hungarian Empire gravely threatened, by the corrosive influence of the national idea. As Sir Lewis Namier said:

The year 1848 marks, for good or evil, the opening of the era of linguistic nationalisms shaping mass personalities and producing their inevitable conflicts: a nation which bases its unity on language cannot easily renounce groups of co-nationals intermingled with those of the neighbouring nation; and an alien minority within the State, or an intensely coveted terra irredenta, are both likely to distort the life of the nation, and impair the growth of its civic liberty. The alien community within the disputed borderland, hostile to the State and possibly plotting against it, provokes repressions which are apt to abase the standards of government; while fellow-countrymen across the border awaiting liberation keep up international tensions, which again are destructive of a free civic life. Moreover, the strongly knitted mass formations of the neo-horde are based on positive feelings which keep the nation together; but the negative feelings, which have to be suppressed within the group, turn with increased virulence against "the stranger in our midst," or against the neighbour.[6]

[6] L. B. Namier, *Avenues of History* (London: Hamish Hamilton, 1952), pp. 43–44.

In Germany, the nationalism released by the Revolution became a pathological force which finally consumed the fabric of peace. The cautious rationalism of the nineteenth century could not take account of William II, and what he represented in German history, any more than the men of Versailles could cope with the Russian Revolution of 1917, or the officeholders of the thirties—it would be an abuse of language to call them statesmen —with Hitler.

The war of 1914–18 was fought to its bitter end, and again, as in 1815, a new world emerged, a mutation of the old one, recognizable, but deeply different. The idea of regarding Europe and the civilized world as "one great republic," "an invisible nation," "a single political system," so dear to Gibbon, Rousseau, and Vattel, and to the Allies of 1815, was expressed symbolically in the League of Nations. Its emergence represented the attraction of the idea to men whose yearning for peace had been heightened by the sickening experience of the war. It represented too the impact on the modern mind of a century-long effort by advocates of "A League to Keep the Peace"—a current in the formation of opinion quite as strong as the advocacy of abolition and of rights for women.

Something was missing during these crucial years, especially in Britain and the United States. Our public life lacked an essential quality—nerve, perhaps; the sense of responsibility and command; and above all an insight into the process of history, which our diffuse educational system rarely encourages. Some of the finest men our culture produces were at the helm at various times during this period—Charles Evans Hughes and Henry L. Stimson, for example. They were as paralyzed, and as mistaken in their assessment of events, as their counterparts in Britain and their colleagues of lesser reputation at home.

Mr. Hughes was a great Chief Justice, and a most distinguished governor, politician, and civic leader. As Secretary of State, he was a disaster. He achieved a treaty limiting naval armaments, which helped to facilitate the military development of

Japan. So far as Europe and the League were concerned, he pursued a course of complete isolation, which repudiated the policy of cooperation with the League he had earlier called a test of his party's "sincerity, integrity and statesmanship."

Similarly, Henry L. Stimson was one of the splendid men of this time—courageous, perceptive, and generous of spirit. As Secretary of State for President Hoover, he had to deal with Japanese aggression in China. All that is left of that fiasco, which led straight to Pearl Harbor, is the doctrine of nonrecognition with which we have deceived ourselves and plagued our foreign policy ever since.

President Roosevelt was surely a giant among our Presidents. It must be admitted, however, that his errors were on the scale of the man himself. It is hard to contend that the state of public opinion, and the legacy of the First World War, made it impossible for him to have moved sooner and more effectively to prevent the Second World War. Could he have used his great prestige after the election of 1936 to lead the United States into the League of Nations, rather than to engage in a bitter and destructive skirmish with the Supreme Court? He might have tried.

These instances do no more than scratch the surface of the problem. One should also recall at least those well-meaning and high-minded men who opposed conscription, both in Britain and the United States, even on the eve of war, and vehemently objected to Britain or the United States entering into the kind of advance political and military commitments that could have prevented the war.

In this realm, as in so many others, innocence is not enough. The frequent recollection of British and American diplomacy in the period between the wars should be an effective remedy against hubris, the sin which all systems of theology place first.

This bitter memory is in considerable part the source of French protest against American and Anglo-American leadership in the Western Alliance since 1945. Being proved right in the event is not an easy satisfaction, especially when the event is immense and the cost so dear. Neither confidence nor enthusiasm is inspired in French minds by the realization that unimaginable tragedy could have been prevented, in 1939 as in 1914, if only Britain and the United States had followed French advice.

The new states' system launched at Versailles lacked the will and the insight to prevail. France and Britain had lost the confidence with which they had exercised authority in the previous century. For a decade or more, Europe was absorbed in seeking to restore societies which had been gravely hurt by the trauma of war. And France could not persuade Britain or the United States to accept its all-too-realistic analysis of the problem of peace. Both Russia and the United States, potentially the largest constellations of power in the postwar world, were isolated from direct participation in European and world politics between 1919 and 1939.

The United States repudiated responsibility, betraying both its allies and its national interests. For twenty years, we pursued a vacuous and nearly suicidal foreign policy of self-righteous neutrality.

In 1917, the government of Russia had suffered a fatal touch of weakness and pathology at the top. It was incapable of steering the nation through the crises precipitated by military defeat. In a situation of crumbling order, a Communist *coup d'état* was assisted by Germany, and succeeded in capturing and consolidating power. The threat of Communism in Italy and Eastern Europe was the occasion for installing more or less totalitarian regimes, which often consciously imitated the Communists in imitating the police methods and the terror of the French Revolution. During the Depression of the thirties, the disease spread to Germany and to Spain.

These dismal events made the system of world politics between 1919 and 1940 almost unmanageable. The emergence of the United States and the Soviet Union as massive centers of military strength altered the balance of ultimate power in the world, and hence the problem of maintaining an equilibrium of peace. Firm and parallel political efforts by the Soviet Union and the United States could have imposed order in Europe, or at least imposed limits on its turbulence. Such policies, however, were unthinkable during the twenties and thirties. Under the circumstances, the same result could have been achieved if Britain had supported France and France's allies in Eastern Europe, and especially if the United States had backed such a policy, during the decade before 1939.

But there was no one in high place capable of preventing what Churchill has rightly called "The Unnecessary War" of 1939–45. The Anglo-French Entente Cordiale of the early twentieth century had ceased to be a rule of policy. For different reasons, we and the Soviets were not at the center of events. And Europe was governed by inadequates or psychopaths.

CHAPTER 3

The Truman Doctrine and World Law, 1945–1963

AT THE END of the Second World War, the world once again confronted the problem of 1648, 1815, and 1919—to establish a reasonably stable constitutional structure for the society of nation states. But this time the United States had to take the lead in the effort.

In this process, the American people confronted a challenge totally new to our national experience. The transformation of world politics has required the United States, like many other nations, to undertake a political mutation, a change in outlook and in conduct which has precipitated a genuine crisis of national identity.

The war had scarcely ended when we began to perceive the magnitude of the burden which history had thrust upon us.

In 1945, many of us looked forward to a harmonious world, organized around a cooperative relationship with the Soviet Union, our associate in the war against Hitler. We tended to conceive of the United Nations as the principal forum in which such cooperation would be effected.

We soon discovered that this hope was a dream. The Soviet Union refused to cooperate with us. It turned down our several offers of aid for reconstruction—including that of the Marshall Plan—and rejected the Baruch Plan for the international control of nuclear energy. Its veto brutally frustrated the United Nations as a peace-keeping agency. Slowly and steadily, it began to thrust outward from its borders. Within a few years, it was joined in uneasy alliance by a Communist China.

For the first time in our history, we had to protect our national security by helping to organize and preserve a world balance of power. Until 1945, we thought such labors were for other nations, less virtuous than we. Now—in a world where Communist power reached out from its bases in the Soviet Union, and then from China; a world where Western Europe was withdrawing from Asia, Africa, and the Middle East, to be succeeded by a large number of weak and vulnerable new nations—in this new world of kaleidoscopic instability we saw that unless we took the lead there was no possibility of organizing the conditions for a durable peace. In magnitude, the effort was beyond the capacity of the nations of Europe. Huge new powers had emerged; later they were to become nuclear powers. If we did not act, no one else could. And if we failed, we should perforce become a garrison state, hemmed in, restrained—hardly the open, confident America we knew and wished to preserve.

The changes in the pattern of world politics have forced many peoples to live through difficult reorientations. They all have the same psychological content. They require nations to give up cherished visions of self, rooted in rich historical experience, and to accept new roles, and new functions, in the light of new and unfamiliar configurations of world power.

It is extraordinarily difficult to escape from the historical memories—from what Jung called the collective unconscious—that shape our sense of ourselves. The effort requires an unequal battle between reason and feeling, between dream and reality. The British and the French are engaged in such an effort—adjusting themselves to the end of empire, and to the new scale of world affairs. So are many other peoples, who find themselves in an altogether new relationship to their neighbors and to the outside world.

Our identity crisis is among the most stubborn of all those which are in process throughout the world. Our collective unconscious is an idyllic vision of America alone, isolated and miraculously safe because we are uniquely blessed—e *pluribus unum*, the chosen people, secure because we are good.

Our four Presidents since 1945 have had to challenge this vision head-on. They have witnessed its irrelevance to the problem of national security, and have been scourged by the angry protest of fellow citizens who preferred to believe that the world is flat. The clash between past and future has stirred the national mind. Neither our educational system nor our history as a nation has prepared our people for the effort to accept the reality of our circumstance.

Until 1914, we could and did ignore the problem of national security. To all intents and purposes, we had no foreign policy, save at the edge of events. We lived in a reasonably stable world, where the balance of power was maintained by the principal European nations. That balance prevented any single country from achieving in the Old World a position of dominance that might threaten our security in the New. And through the system of empire it organized a pattern of general peace for the world as a whole.

American public opinion was unaware of the forces guarding our security. A professor would have been hooted down for pointing out that the safety of the Republic depended on the British fleet. And a politician's career would have come to an end if he had been suspected of such a subversive thought. In the American language, "the balance of power" was a reactionary idea, evoking all that was evil in imperialism. Our schools and colleges, and the larger part of the literature which influenced public opinion, helped to deepen our attachment to illusion.

The tradition of isolation, enshrined in President Washington's famous Farewell, is a powerful part of our collective memory.

It is reinforced as an influence by a related strain in our culture, a naïve Utopianism that is the dark side of our idealism. America has always been rich in True Believers—zealots of one stripe or another, who were convinced that the world could be restored to its innocence if only we adopted the Single Tax, or lived on Brook Farm, or gave up eating meat. They had comparably realistic views on problems of peace. The Utopians have always imagined that the world is naturally harmonious, and that the freedom of every man to do as he pleases would lead naturally to a peaceful order. Men dreamed of carving such a world from the abundant and uncorrupted American wilderness. On the real frontier, however, we quickly learned the lesson of *High Noon*—that without organized power to maintain the law, freedom is impossible.

But the Utopian ideal, which had no place in national politics, reappeared in the common American vision of the international world—an unknown universe, where only a few Americans had occasional business. The view developed that peace was normal, or rather would be normal if we replaced the immoral practices of diplomacy and "power politics" by the rules of a new, pure international body—a true Parliament of Man.

No one remarked the irony of that outlook for a people whose sense of power in their domestic politics is so acute. After all, our Constitution is a hyper-refined system of checks and balances, intended to curb power in the interest of freedom. But until recently, when we thought about foreign affairs at all, most of us believed that the world's order and our liberty were gifts of nature rather than accomplishments of men.

The historical conditions which promoted these illusions came to an end in 1917. Belatedly we intervened in the First World War to prevent a threatening hegemony in Europe. But after the war we took refuge in the past—as soon as possible, and all too soon. All through the 1920's and 1930's, our isolationism kept America from doing what was necessary to protect its own security. As a result, Hitler's power could not be contained: our influence in world affairs was not felt in time to prevent the Second World War.

By 1945, the Concert of Europe had gone the way of Humpty Dumpty. It had prevented general war for a century before 1914. But the nations of Europe were exhausted by two wars, and by the tragedies and follies of the years between the wars. Vast new powers and new political forces were emerging in the world. Russia, China, Japan, and the United States were countries on a new scale. The nuclear weapon had been born. Time had transformed the problem of equilibrium. It was altogether beyond the reach of the old entente.

We came to understand, but not quite to accept, the fact that, in the small, unstable nuclear world in which we have no choice but to live, the security of the United States depends on maintaining a tolerably stable balance of power not merely in the Western Atlantic, in Europe, and in the Hemisphere, but in the world as a whole. And we began to perceive as well that if the security of the United States was to be protected we were going to have to undertake a major part of the job ourselves. There was no one else. In President Truman's phrase, "The buck stops here."

This fact has determined both the tasks we have had to undertake abroad since the war, and the recurrent spasms of domestic political conflict we have experienced in facing them.

Since 1945, having been drawn into two world wars, we have recognized our national interest in the balance of world power. At the level of reason, we now know that any major war will necessarily involve us, and that any considerable disturbance in the equilibrium of affairs will threaten our sense of security. We have come finally to understand that we can protect the security of the United States only by actively participating in world politics. Our national interest in that process is to help preserve peace in a realm of ample horizons—a realm ample enough, and dynamic enough, to accommodate the changing policies of many free peoples without losing the discipline of peace.

In this period our foreign policy has had to deal with three streams of events—separate in one sense, interrelated in another.

One-third of the world's population has come under the control of ambitious and energetic Communist regimes. Two of them now possess nuclear weapons. They are no longer united in a common discipline. But on some issues they still come together. Separately and as a group, they have probed our defenses, and tested our will. Despite setbacks, these efforts at expansion continue.

Another third of the world's people live in developing countries. Many of them have achieved freedom from imperial tutelage during this period. They are all groping their way toward modernity under conditions of relative weakness which tempt aggression.

The rest of the world consists of the advanced and industrialized free nations. For a large part of the period since 1945, Britain, France, the Netherlands, and Belgium have engaged in the complex process of decolonization and withdrawal from their former positions of influence and responsibility in many parts of the world. That adjustment has involved severe psychological costs. Germany, Italy, and Japan have been absorbed in their successful recovery from the bitter experience of tyranny and war. It is not remarkable that the advanced nations as a group, barely restored after these difficult transitions, have been unable as yet fully to concert their influence with ours in the quest for stability and progress outside of Europe itself.

In the first few years after the war, as we began to perceive the impact of these flows of change on our security, some thought we could establish conditions of order exclusively or principally through the United Nations. Many hoped that it would become a new world system in which peace and our own security would be guarded through the collective action of the Great Powers, and of the world community at large. But the United Nations was not designed to function as a peace-keeping body when the Great Powers disagreed, and it could not be made to do so.

Thus we turned to the classic methods of diplomacy, and sought to build stability through regional coalitions of like-minded powers, coalitions designed to deter Soviet- or Chinese-supported aggression and to give war-ravaged and newly independent states time to build the strength that would end or reduce their vulnerability.

When the Soviet Union breached the Yalta and Potsdam agreements calling for free elections in Eastern Europe and Germany, and began to push outward toward Iran, Turkey, and Greece, our response, in 1947, was the Truman Doctrine and the Marshall Plan. Together these policies embody the two complementary principles of our postwar foreign policy: military security and peaceful progress.

We knew that neither policy could succeed without the other. There could be no permanent security without progress toward a better social order, but no progress in a world of fear where aggression was frequent and successful, and mankind was burdened by an arms race.

President Truman stated the essence of his doctrine in this way:

> To ensure the peaceful development of nations, free from coercion, the United States has taken a leading part in establishing the United Nations. The United Nations is designed to make possible lasting freedom and independence for all its members. We shall not realize our objectives, however, unless we are willing to help free peoples to maintain their free institutions and their national integrity against aggressive movements that seek to impose upon them totalitarian regimes. This is no more than a frank recognition that totalitarian regimes imposed upon free peoples, by direct or indirect aggression, undermine the foundations of international peace and hence the security of the United States.

For twenty years, this principle has been the cement of the world, and its hope of peace. In Europe, it became the basis of NATO, the solid and powerful Atlantic Alliance which has been the cornerstone of our security and foreign policy. Comparable arrangements of alliance have developed slowly in some other regions of the world.

In effect, President Truman said, "Thus far, and no farther." The Truman Doctrine did not recognize a division of the world into spheres of influence. It did not suspend the rules of the Charter against aggression for countries under Communist control. As President Kennedy pointed out to a Russian audience in 1961, the world has not forgotten the promises of freedom in Eastern Europe which the Soviet Union made at Yalta and at Potsdam. Détente can hardly be imagined until those promises are kept.

In 1947, President Truman was dealing with a different problem—the use of American force to protect the American national interest. He was drawing a line to preserve the possibility of equilibrium, and to prevent any further change in the balance of forces. He invoked the threat of military force to arrest the process of Communist expansion, so that political methods might have an opportunity to achieve genuine peace.

During these years of rising and falling tension, the Truman Doctrine has gradually evolved, first in Europe and then in Asia, into a kind of common law of international order, a prudent rule of reciprocal safety. It is a simple rule, and therefore minimizes uncertainty and miscalculation. I should put it this way: equilibrium, and therefore the possibility of détente, requires mutual understanding that neither side should attempt to change the frontiers of the systems by force or by the threat of force. For such attempts, unlike certain other forms of change, threaten the general world equilibrium, and therefore risk a confrontation between great powers, and world war.

The Truman Doctrine does not require us and our allies to be the universal policemen of the world. There are many conflicts in the world which do not involve the risk of confrontation with the Soviet Union or with Communist China, or otherwise threaten our national interests, or the balance of power. But it has required us and our allies to make extraordinary efforts in many parts of the world in our effort to obtain the acceptance of the principle of live-and-let-live.

Our political and military moves during this period were by no means neat and precise. They represented the gropings of earnest men in response to inchoate dangers, often dimly perceived, not the execution of neat plans, prepared in advance.

But events have had a pattern. Our actions correspond to a policy—that of seeking to achieve a system of peace through which we and our allies could rationally hope for détente between the Communist and the non-Communist states. It has not been a policy of crusade. Nor has policy rested on the illusion of American omnipotence. No one has dreamed of undoing the Bolshevik Revolution in the Soviet Union, or of conquering China. Nor have we sought to remake the world in the American political image. All we have sought, and used limited power to achieve, is the acceptance by the Communist nations of a rule of order— an organized and accepted pattern of peace.

Our foreign policy and our public opinion have had to grapple with a series of problems novel to our modes of thought.

For example, we have had to learn to distinguish between actions in the national interest and actions in support of governments we approved. Some Americans find it nearly inconceivable that national security interests might make it necessary for us to cooperate with dictatorial governments, or that the United States cannot always (or often) persuade foreign governments to adopt constitutions like our own.

It is always a mistake to think of the United States as a conservative influence. As children of 1776, we approved of movements for freedom within the colonial empires, and almost always opted for decolonization against security, even though that choice required us to oppose the policies of our closest allies. The same sense of connection with a revolutionary tradition has complicated our reaction to military efforts that called themselves revolutionary in Greece, in China, in Cuba and in Vietnam. Our first instinct is to assist regimes which purport to identify themselves with the hopes and aspirations of the masses, and keep our distance from dictatorial governments, or those dominated by privileged groups. In the beginning, we supported Sukarno, Nkrumah, and Nasser with high expectations, and we were ready to assist Castro as well. And of course we supported the Soviet Union under Stalin during the war against Hitler, although many did so in the grip of illusions about the "liberal" character of Stalin's regime.

In the second place, it is equally difficult for many of us to accept the idea that the principle of the Truman Doctrine is reciprocal. It requires that we ourselves respect the vital interests of the Communist nations. In this connection, one should recall our refusal to intervene when trouble occurred in Czechoslovakia, in 1948; in East Germany, in 1953; or in Hungary, in 1956. And, for the same basic reasons, neither we nor our NATO allies undertook nuclear war to prevent or repel the Soviet invasion of Czechoslovakia in 1968. But Communist leaders have not exercised a similar respect for the interests of the non-Communist world. The Truman Doctrine has been put to the test in a long cycle of episodes, from Iran and Berlin to Korea and Vietnam. Sometimes, as in Korea, Communist efforts at conquest have involved the United States and some of her allies in limited wars. On other occasions, like efforts elsewhere brought the whole world to the edge of nuclear war, most notably perhaps in the Cuban missile crisis of 1962.

Throughout this period, however, there grew up a certain precarious stability. It became more and more apparent that the two rival super-powers had become linked in a marriage not of convenience but of necessity, a relationship which dominated their ideological antipathies, and their occasional conflicts of interest as national states.

At some level of consciousness, the leaders of the Soviet Union must appreciate the fact that we did not attempt to use our atomic monopoly between 1945 and the early fifties, either to end Communist rule in the Soviet Union or to prevent the Communist takeovers in China and in Eastern Europe. Certain Soviet leaders have undoubtedly thought we were stupid and short-sighted not to do so. But as a group they must acknowledge this cardinal fact about the postwar world as evidence of our peaceful purpose.

After twenty years, it became possible to speak of a "special relation" between the United States and the Soviet Union, perhaps the most important of the "special relations" maintained by either. Of course, all relations between pairs of countries are "special," colored by particular aspects of the past and the future. The central feature of the present-day relationship between the United States and the Soviet Union is symbolized by the "hot line" installed after the Cuban missile crisis of 1962. The two countries are the custodians of decisive military power in the contemporary world. They have shared responsibility for avoiding the unthinkable disaster of another World War; even more important, they have realized the fact. The strange vision of a Soviet-American peace, first visible during the Suez crisis of 1956, has been manifest on several subsequent occasions as the final counterweight for order.

The relationship between the Soviet Union and the United States comprises many threads. In part—in large part—it is a relationship between the United States and Russia, the huge, cautious, growing nation destined, as Tocqueville saw, to be a great power coeval with the American giant during the twentieth century—ancient Russia, Holy Russia, a nation with its own historical style of international action, the heir of Alexander's dreams and Peter's, as well as those of Ivan the Terrible and of Stalin. The Russian policy includes, inevitably, the consequences of the Bolshevik Revolution, and the capture of authority by the party of Lenin and Trotsky. Like all of Russia, that party lives in a state of unresolved tension between its Western and Eastern outlooks, between St. Petersburg and Moscow, between Chekhov and Dostoevsky. That conflict has often been portrayed, never more vividly than in the secondary plot of *Anna Karenina*.

46

American public opinion has always favored a fair understanding with the Soviet Union. In the late forties, we wanted to continue our wartime association with the Russian people and with the Soviet Union. We had fresh memories of wartime comradeship in arms, of hands across the Elbe, of the Soviet contribution to the victory over Hitler. We recalled other ties and similarities between our two peoples: the traits of generosity, of spontaneity, and of frankness which both peoples like to call their own. We recalled, too, that both peoples had undergone the invigorating experience of everything conjured up by the idea of "the frontier": the great westward expansion of our own country paralleled the eastward expansion of the Russian people. We appreciated Russian literature, music, and theatre; and the Russians found much to admire in the works of many American writers.

There was also, let us not forget, much genuine sympathy in the United States for the March Revolution of 1917 and for the ideals which it proclaimed. There was more than a little initial sympathy for the October Revolution as well.

And, finally, we had a practical awareness of the importance of the Soviet Union and respect for its power. We had begun to understand that the future of world peace would depend on the relationship established by the two giants, and that a unique mutual responsibility bound the two nations together.

The oriental theme in Russian policy was in the ascendant at the end of the war. But while the men who governed the Soviet Union may sometimes have been tempted to recall that the Communist movement had made its principal gains in situations of chaos and disorganization after prolonged wars, they have been too cautious, and too concerned with Russian national interests, to risk war with the United States in their efforts to spread Communism by the sword. They have probed, and put us to severe tests, like those of Korea and Vietnam. But thus far, at least, they have drawn back from direct confrontation in areas beyond the borders of 1945. So long as the United States and its allies retain sufficient military power to constitute credible deterrence, American policy has been able to rest on the assumption that the Soviet Union will pursue a course at least as prudent as that of the last twenty years.

In the thrusts and responses of these twenty years, it has often been possible to hope that the governors of the Soviet Union had come to understand that the policies of the United States were hardly those of "aggressive imperialism" regularly described in Communist oratory, but something tractable and conciliatory, and far less threatening. The two countries, it has sometimes seemed, had come to know that their shared trusteeship of military power was the ultimate guaranty of general peace.

The potentialities of Soviet-American cooperation for peace were dramatized in the settlement of the India-Pakistan War in 1963. But, while hope grew for a peace based on such cooperation, the world was evolving toward a new and more complex pattern which called that hope into question. The development of Soviet naval and air power, and the refinement of techniques of indirect or proxy war—in wars of "national liberation" or in situations like that of the Middle East—may signal a new era of more intense Cold War. Thus far, this is a possibility to be taken into account, rather than a postulate of policy.

The Soviet-American duopoly of power was ending, at least in the political sense, and we seemed to be entering an era in which the principal threats to peace could no longer be defined exclusively as Soviet or Chinese aggression, nor contained successfully by Russian-American cooperation, however painfully achieved. New powers have arisen in the world and old powers have revived. New styles of aggression have emerged—proxy wars and wars of national liberation. They become threats to the general peace only when they are supported by Soviet or Chinese power.

The result of this new fragmentation of power is clear today in Vietnam, where the force of a tacit Soviet-American link seems no longer to be enough, as it was after Suez or Korea, or during the brief war between India and Pakistan, to bring hostilities to an end, and restore something like order. Aid to North Vietnam by the Soviet Union and the nations of Eastern Europe is a phenomenon of ideology. It cannot be explained in terms of Soviet or East European national interests. Soviet policy in the Middle East has comparable, if not parallel features.

The situation of the last few years has posed an increasingly serious challenge to the precarious world order built up around the Truman Doctrine.

This challenge, in turn, has stirred a new revolt in American opinion against the realities and burdens of the twentieth century.

Our confrontation with these linked processes of change is the essence of our foreign policy in the Johnson Administration. The one clear lesson that emerges is that in a multipolar world the Truman Doctrine can only be maintained as the constituent principle of an emergent world order by a broad coalition of forces responsibly interested in preventing a breakdown of the nascent world system. The problem of peace in the late 1960's depends on a modification of the equation which has proved so realistic for twenty years. More than ever, the goal of "peaceful coexistence" requires the powerful industrial nations of the Free World to combine their influence in the interest of stability and peaceful progress. But if such a genuine concert is to develop, there must be fundamental alterations in the relations between us and our allies.

The passage of time, inevitably, has made the NATO pattern of 1949 obsolete. New modes of organizing the Atlantic Alliance are essential, if it is not to break. Basic changes in the underlying condition of states and peoples now require the postwar trusteeship of the United States to become in fact the system of concert for which it was conceived as a temporary substitute. In its earlier postwar form, the American protectorate has become politically unacceptable both in Europe and in the United States. The same transformation of protectorate into partnership is essential in the relationship between the United States and Japan, and between the United States and other countries, if the political base for American responsibility is to be preserved and strengthened. In every perspective, regional coalitions of free nations built around American nuclear power remain the indispensable base and precondition of world peace.

CHAPTER 4

New Challenges to American
Foreign Policy, 1963–1968

WHEN PRESIDENT JOHNSON came into office in 1963, both the world and American opinion were in transition. On the surface the weather seemed relatively clear. But storms were brewing and soon became manifest. In many respects, the last five years have been the most difficult yet faced by our postwar foreign policy. And the return to an atmosphere of danger has revived latent American yearnings to escape into our isolationist past—the most powerful such wave of feeling since 1920, when we repudiated Wilson and accepted the empty promises of President Harding.

The simultaneous revival of foreign and domestic pressure has constituted a formidable challenge to our foreign policy. The main positions of American foreign policy had been firmly articulated by 1963. They had been constant since the first hesitant months after the end of the Second World War. Together, they frame a policy four Presidents and a bipartisan majority of the American people have found necessary to make our democracy safe in the world as it is. The chief themes of that policy can be simply stated: containment and the steady pursuit of détente; support for the Atlantic Alliance, the European movement, and alliance with Japan; decolonization and aid to the developing nations; a liberal trade policy; international monetary cooperation in the interest of growth and full employment; arms limitation; the control of nuclear weapons. Together, these policies constitute a strategy for building a new world system—a system that could translate the Truman Doctrine into a universally accepted rule against aggression, and release the impulses of progress among all peoples.

On the basis of this moderate and restrained idea, it was reasonable to hope, the Soviet Union and Communist China might be persuaded to accept policies of coexistence. Containment could give way to peace.

When the President took office in 1963, that strategy could look back on considerable success. American policy since 1945 had interposed powerful arrangements of protection to deter Communist attempts to extend their spheres of control. In addition, the United States had sponsored and had participated in various regional and international programs of economic assistance. Much had been achieved by these efforts. Europe and Japan were flourishing. And many of the nonindustrialized countries had begun to succeed in their development efforts. All had come to realize that success was possible.

In 1963, then, one could discern the possibilities of order in the world—the kind and degree of order required for our security as a world power, equally involved in the Atlantic and the Pacific. But it was clear too that it was still a world of many risks.

The European states, stripped of their empires, were withdrawing from Asia, Africa, and the Middle East. They had not yet succeeded in forming a political Europe, through which they could join the United States as an equal partner in all the works of peace. Under these circumstances, some Europeans found irresponsibility tempting. As their economic strength and political confidence increased, they grew restive at alliance arrangements drawn up during the years of their weakness and dependence. Meanwhile, Japan, brilliantly successful in its postwar recovery, was only beginning her re-entry into world politics as our colleague and ally. These developments were bound to demand an eventual redefinition of our mutual relations and responsibilities.

At the same time, the developing countries, not yet strong enough to withstand attack, generated conflicts of their own, and tempted intervention by one sect or another of the Communist world. Economic development was proving at best to be a slow and painful process. For many countries the social transformations were cruel—particularly in traditionalist societies for which modern technology seems an alien and often an unwelcome intrusion. Increasing prosperity does not always bring social peace, as we in the West have good reason to know. In all these troubled waters, it was not surprising to find the Communists fishing, along with others, hoping to profit from disorder.

It is absurd to imagine that all the trouble in the world is inspired by Communists. But it is equally absurd to suppose that Communists are not serious men, seriously committed to their creed. It is too much to suppose that they will be more virtuous than other human beings in resisting temptation. They will be found where the fabric of order is weakest. Thus, it is not accident that in President Johnson's Administration the most acute problems of foreign policy have arisen in Southeast Asia and the Middle East, two areas where the end of empire has left weak states, vulnerable to direct or indirect takeover by Communist power.

Indeed, in both these areas, prolonged crises have developed, crises which threaten the equilibrium of power in the world as a whole, and therefore create the risk of general war. Each has involved not only local conflicts among small quarreling neighbors, but, at one remove, the relationship between the United States and the Soviet Union, and, to a certain extent, that between both these powers and Communist China as well.

These confrontations have posed a new threat to the Truman Doctrine. Indeed they call into question all that has been achieved since the war in building a stable international order. In many respects, these threats are more difficult to meet than visible and dramatic challenges, like the several attempts to blockade Berlin, or the missile crisis in Cuba, which were open and direct confrontations of super-powers whose implications could not be hidden. President Johnson's tests in Vietnam and the Near East are of a different order. They go on, month after month, taut and menacing. But they occur in circumstances which make comparative silence prudent. Their limits are determined by the clarity with which we define our essential purposes and prepare the way for peaceful settlement.

The Johnson Administration has had to face not only an intensification of threats abroad, but also the most serious isolationist challenge to our postwar foreign policy since the outcry about Korea which led President Truman not to run in 1952.

Why should such an attack have occurred in this period? What are the views that lie behind it?

For many Americans, the international exertions we have had to undertake since 1945 have been accepted as temporary and transitional efforts. They tend to think the First World War was an aberration, and the Second a unique phenomenon caused by Hitler. If we did a good enough job with the Marshall Plan and aid programs, and fended off aggression in Berlin, Greece, and Korea, the Soviets and the Chinese would come to believe in the reasonableness of peaceful coexistence; Europe, the Middle East, and Asia would recover their capacity to defend themselves; then we could bring the boys home, and return to "normalcy."

The Presidency of Lyndon B. Johnson marks the end of these illusions. We see that the world we have known since 1945 is not a temporary period of postwar disturbance, but our normal condition, at least until rules of peaceful coexistence can be accepted, and new groupings formed to guarantee them. And we realize now that it will take a long time and a great deal of patient, restrained effort to create a system that might effectively maintain order in a world that contains so many breeding grounds for hostility and violence.

This is the root of the revulsion of public opinion about Vietnam which President Johnson had to confront. Other aspects of the war in Vietnam heightened the feeling of revulsion: the distaste for bombing as a form of warfare, and for any contest between a small country and a big one. But the decisive element in American concern about Vietnam is resistance to the bleak fact with which President Johnson lived every day of his term: the fact that the protection of our national security requires not a sprint, a one-shot effort, followed by the relief of a withdrawal, but a permanent involvement in the politics of every part of the globe, based on a strategy of peace that seeks to achieve order and to make progress possible.

In one context after another, the American people have been caught up in this tension between history and the facts of life ever since President Wilson called on us to join the League of Nations in 1919. In times of stress, we yearn for the comfort and security of the nineteenth century. Then, we imagine, Americans lived in a Golden Age, when the country was more completely devoted to the austere virtues, and giants walked the earth.

With our minds, we understand that the nineteenth century is gone beyond recall, and indeed that our vision of the past is myth. But the outlook of those easy times is deep in our psyche. And our educational system does not give most Americans the feel for history which would equip them to understand the problem of power without a special effort. For these reasons, the debate has been protracted and difficult to resolve. There are still respected and high-minded American leaders who contend that our main contribution to world order should be the power of our example as a model society at home.

Put in these terms, the debate heightens confusion by posing a choice between an effective foreign policy and social progress at home. The larger part of our people are committed to the ideal of social progress. They also understand the necessities of power which require us in our own interest to help safeguard the general peace. Between these goals, there need in fact be no choosing. The state of public opinion, and the strength of the nation, permit us to pursue both.

But the confusion has a deeper element than the question of choice. Nowadays, the goal of social improvement is to eliminate violence in social life, and to make progress toward social justice. As we slowly advance toward that ideal, after nearly one hundred and eighty years of effort, we confront an obligation to use or to threaten violence abroad on a much larger scale than ever before in our history, violence repugnant to all that is best in our aspiration for ourselves. No wonder troubled men ask themselves whether Revolutionary America has become an imperial power, taking over the role of the Redcoats, whether Republican America must now support kings and dictators.

The argument between these two parts of the American mind has proceeded in stages. In the twenties, it focused on our membership in the League of Nations. Ten years later, it asked whether German and Japanese militarism really threatened our national safety. Twenty years ago, in the days of Henry Wallace and Senator Joseph McCarthy, it was directed to the Truman Doctrine, the Marshall Plan, and the hostilities in Korea. Today the nominal topic for debate is our involvement in Vietnam—whether that conflict genuinely concerns our national interests, and above all our national interest in the balance of power.

But every round of the debate has been in fact part of a more fundamental effort to free our minds of obsolete dogmas about ourselves and the world. The true issue at each stage has been the ultimate question: why do we have to be involved at all?

To that question the facts permit only one answer: the alternative of isolation is not available to the American people, now or for the foreseeable future. The patient, long-range campaigns of President Johnson's foreign policy have all been addressed to this assessment of reality.

President Johnson's foreign policy extends and applies that of his predecessors to changing circumstance. But on many fronts his sense of strategy has carried policy beyond the past.

The essential idea of his foreign policy has been to use the power of the United States as the magnetic center of several overlapping systems of international cooperation. Together, coalitions of this kind can counterbalance destructive tendencies, and provide a framework for stability and progress in the several regions of the world, and in the world as a whole.

The world system to which we aspire is not a sterile program of order for its own sake, achieved by coercion and maintained only by force. Peace and progress are dependent on each other. And most Americans are enthusiastic devotees of progress. We want nothing more than to help build a world in which man could enjoy the blessings of liberty and seek to overcome his burdens of hunger, ignorance, and ill-health through a process of political development toward self-government. That vision of the purpose of America in the world is fundamental to our nature.

But the United States has not been engaged in an ideological crusade, either to extirpate one or another form of Communism, or to transform the whole Free World in the model of American democracy. The aim of our foreign policy is to protect our national interest in world stability. Of course the United States encourages the development of democratic institutions, and the pursuit of economic and social progress, wherever we can exert our influence to do so. That fact, however, is the consequence of our involvement, not its cause. The end we seek is a tolerably stable system of peace in world politics, achieved in collaboration with other nations, and sustained with their consent and support—a system of diversity, in the spirit of the United Nations Charter, "based on respect for the principle of equal rights and self-determination of peoples,"—above all, a system of peace.

The process of world politics which faces us is a race between fission and fusion, between the forces which tend to fragment the world and those which work toward harmony. The nations are drawn together by common interests, common values, and common fears. They are driven apart by pride, fear, suspicion, ignorance of each other's motives, and the power of aggressive instincts.

Despite fluctuations of American opinion, policy has remained remarkably consistent in response to pressures which have also been remarkably consistent. In this, the United States has confounded the philosophers of politics, who have always thought that a democracy is incapable of a sustained foreign policy, because public opinion, they think, is so fickle. Presidents Truman and Johnson stoically accepted their tribulations as foreordained. As happens sometimes to prime ministers in a parliamentary system, they have been sacrificed to popular frustration, without requiring a change in policy. Our Presidents and Secretaries of State in this period have not been victims of false optimism. They have never enjoyed a moment when their foreign policy was popular. But they have persevered, confident that in the end the strength and high purpose of American policy, and the sober second thoughts of the American people, would provide the margin of influence ultimately needed to achieve a system of peace.

CHAPTER 5

The Major Tests, Vietnam
and the Middle East

IN RECENT YEARS, the United States has had to face major threats to the peace both in Southeast Asia and in the Middle East. In both instances, the concern of policy has been to protect American interests and world stability without risking general war.

President Johnson's policy in South Vietnam has two essential features: restraint in the use of force and maximum diplomatic effort toward political conciliation.

In the Near East, of course, American force has not been applied, although the possibility of its use has been the controlling factor moving the crisis toward a peaceful resolution. In a wide-ranging process of diplomatic consultation, the full weight of American influence has steadfastly pressed to bring the parties and their friends to accept a definitive political settlement of the Arab-Israeli conflict and final Arab acceptance of Israel's right to live.

The International Politics of Vietnam

The situation in Southeast Asia which President Johnson inherited in 1963 was not without hope, if the Soviet Union could be persuaded to cooperate in enforcing the agreements for the neutralization of Laos it had made with us the year before. But that hope, like so many others, proved illusory.

The basic elements of the problem are well known, but they bear restatement.

The Geneva agreements of 1954 undertook to end the hostilities in Indochina and make it possible for the peoples of that area to develop their independence in peace. The Vietminh was to withdraw its forces from Laos and Cambodia, and from the area south of the seventeenth parallel in Vietnam. French Union forces were to withdraw from Vietnam north of the seventeenth parallel. For Laos and Cambodia, this amounted to recognition of the existing royal governments as the sole legal authorities. For Vietnam, in effect, the agreement meant that in the northern zone Ho Chi Minh's Democratic Republic of Vietnam became the de facto government. In the southern zone, Emperor Bao Dai's State of Vietnam was able to consolidate its authority. It was then in the final stages of attaining full independence from France and later was to become a republic.

The agreements provided the possibility that North and South Vietnam could be united as a single state if the peoples of both states, through free elections under international supervision, expressed the wish to be reunited. It was also clear, however, that for the time being the two parts of Vietnam were to be distinct political entities, as was the case in Germany and Korea. Provision was made to allow individuals to migrate from one area to the other, in the expectation of a division of the country which some thought might last for a considerable time. The regimes in Saigon and Hanoi were "governments" in every practical sense, exercising the normal authority of governments, although they were not universally recognized.

The United States made certain basic positions explicit in 1954. We were not a party to the Geneva Accords, but we were far from indifferent to their content. It was clear at the time that there were some outcomes we could not accept. Further, we stated that we should view any aggression in violation of the Geneva

60

Accords with concern, as seriously threatening international peace and security. And third, we took the same position on the reunification of South and North Vietnam that we took in regard to other "nations now divided against their will," that is to say, Germany and Korea. Our policy was that in Vietnam, as in Germany and Korea, we should continue to favor unity by peaceful means, and ultimately through free elections supervised by the United Nations, but that reunification through the use of force was inadmissible. It was manifestly impossible in 1956 to hold free elections under international supervision in North Vietnam, where thousands of dissidents had already been liquidated. It was not conceivable that North Vietnam would permit supervision for elections that could be called free. The government of South Vietnam therefore concluded that the referendum provisions of the Geneva Accords could not be carried out as scheduled. The United States acquiesced in this decision, as most responsible observers did under the circumstances. The Soviet Union did not object.

In 1954, we sought to give formal structure to a coalition among ourselves, some of our allies, and a number of the non-Communist states of Southeast Asia. The result was the SEATO Treaty. In that document, we and our allies underwrote the provisions against direct and indirect aggression in the Geneva Accords. The new government of South Vietnam and its territory were expressly protected by a protocol to the SEATO Treaty, which aimed more widely to safeguard the security of the Southeast Asian signatories, and the other successor states of Indochina. Thus the United States was formally committed as guarantor of the peace in Southern Asia, as it had been committed five years earlier in Europe.

These steps derived from President Eisenhower's considered judgment about the nature of American interests in protecting the integrity and assisting the development of the independent nations of Southeast Asia. We undertook these successive obligations for the same reasons which led us to safeguard the security of Japan, Korea, and the Republic of China. As a Pacific power, we have a national security interest in preventing the transfer of the area, or large parts of it, to Communist control achieved by subversion and aggression. Such conquests would mean a major addition to the power status of hostile and aggressive Communist Chinese and North Vietnamese regimes. It would alter the expectations of many other nations, in Asia, in Europe, and in the Middle East, which rely for their security on an American guaranty. And it would doom our plans for constructive political and economic progress toward stability and development in the region.

There is the view, of course, that it is hopeless to intervene in these explosive situations—that Southeast Asia, South America, and Africa are destined to go through revolutionary turmoil of many kinds, and that nothing can be done to stem the flood.

The simplest answer to this opinion is the accomplishments of many developing states, often achieved in the face of threats both from within and without: Iran, for example, and Thailand, Israel, South Korea, Taiwan, and Malaysia. India and Pakistan have made notable advances in recent years, against formidable obstacles. Others, like Indonesia, have turned sharply from adventurism to policies of peace and economic development. All over the world countries are choosing their own paths to development, based upon their national traditions and their perception of the enlightened methods of modern capitalism, which have brought about the social revolutions of the Free World since 1945—by all odds the most progressive and successful revolutions of the century.

South Vietnam, on the other hand, has had little chance. Starting in 1957, or at least in 1959, the government of North Vietnam began systematically to initiate and to support guerrilla hostilities against the government of South Vietnam. That effort, steadily increasing in scale and tempo, was part of a deliberate plan to unite Vietnam by force under Communist domination. Its significance to world politics was exactly the same as if attempts had been made by either side to unify Germany or Korea by force. There, too, after all, unification had been promised through free elections; and there, too, elections had not been held.

By 1961, the guerrilla aggression against South Vietnam had made ominous progress. President Kennedy decided to enlarge the program of political, economic, and military aid which President Eisenhower had started. He increased the number of our military advisers, and sent in pilots and other supporting military personnel to assist the armed forces of the South Vietnamese government. Their number rose gradually to 25,000.

This then was the situation which President Johnson found when he became President: a treaty commitment to protect South Vietnam, made by President Eisenhower and ratified by the Senate, and a process of military participation under that treaty, which had been maintained and greatly strengthened by President Kennedy.

North Vietnam intensified its effort, and, as early as 1964, sent its own regular troops to supplement the guerrilla forces organized, trained, and infiltrated from the North. In the same period, attacks were made directly on American naval vessels in the Tonkin Gulf, and on American installations in South Vietnam. These episodes of escalation took place in 1964—a moment in time when Indonesia, under strong Communist influence, was attacking Malaysia, and recurrent trouble threatened India as well. President Johnson ordered retaliatory action in the Tonkin Gulf, and presented the situation to the Congress.

On August 7, 1964, Congress passed a resolution which not only approved retaliatory action in the Tonkin Gulf but reiterated the basic policy decisions taken since 1954 in asserting America's security interest in the defense of Southeast Asia. The second operative part of the resolution reads as follows:

> The United States regards as vital to its national interest and to world peace the maintenance of international peace and security in South East Asia. Consonant with the Constitution and the Charter of the United Nations and in accordance with its obligations under the South East Collective Defense Treaty, the United States is, therefore, prepared, as the President determines, to take all necessary steps, including the use of armed force, to assist any member or protocol state of the South East

Asia Collective Defense Treaty requesting assistance in defense of its freedom.

The language of that resolution, and the discussion of its meaning in the Congress, make its significance crystal clear. When Congress and the President act together, the full weight of the nation is placed behind policy. In this instance, the position President Eisenhower took at Geneva in 1954, and in the SEATO Treaty, was solemnly reaffirmed. And American military participation in the war in Vietnam was fully authorized. The joint resolution has the same constitutional status, though not the same international and legal consequences, as a joint resolution declaring that a state of war exists.

Early in 1965, President Johnson made the basic decisions to bomb targets in North Vietnam, and to send American troops into combat. It was clear at the time that if he had not taken this step South Vietnam would have fallen. Would such an event have proved the guarantees of the SEATO Treaty worthless? Would the strong Chinese and North Vietnamese threat to Southeast Asia have multiplied in strength?

The President and other spokesmen for the Administration have explained the purpose of our actions in Vietnam on many occasions. The policy was fully stated in President Johnson's speech at Baltimore in April, 1965. We are in Vietnam, he said, for the same reason that we have a responsibility in Europe—because great interests in world order are in balance and therefore our own security is at stake. The "deepening shadow of Communist China" is the reality behind the contest in Vietnam, which "is part of a wider pattern of aggressive intention." We are there, he went on, because "we have a promise to keep," and it would shake confidence "from Berlin to Thailand" if an American commitment were proved worthless.

Our objective is the independence of South Viet-Nam, and its freedom from attack. We want nothing for ourselves—only that the people of South Viet-Nam be allowed to guide their own country in their own way.

We will do everything necessary to reach that objective. And we will do only what is absolutely necessary.

The legal and political basis for our course in Vietnam is clear.

Whatever view one takes of the disputed origins of the war in Vietnam—whether it is considered simply an insurrection against the authority of the South Vietnamese state aided by North Vietnam, or an infiltration and invasion from North Vietnam—the issue of international law and politics is the same. In either view of the facts, North Vietnam is waging war against South Vietnam. And South Vietnam has the right to ask for the help of the international community in resisting the North Vietnamese attack. No state has the right to assist an insurrection against another. The international law on the subject has been agreed for centuries, and it is confirmed by the Charter of the United Nations.

Nor can it be contended for this purpose that all of Vietnam is one country, so that the North Vietnamese attempt to conquer South Vietnam should be considered a civil war, and therefore an internal affair of the Vietnamese nation. The argument proves too much. It would license a unification of Germany and of Korea by force. And it is denied by the facts. There is no Vietnamese state; on the contrary, the two political entities governed from Hanoi and Saigon are in fact separate states, so acknowledged by the international community, by the SEATO Treaty, and by many other acts of recognition. Both regimes raise taxes and armies, conduct foreign relations, and exercise all the normal activities of governments within their boundaries.

Neither South Vietnam nor the United States is interested in conquering North Vietnam, or in overturning its Communist regime. The only issue of the war is whether North Vietnam will be allowed forcibly to impose its system on South Vietnam.

But, men ask, does the United States have any national interest in South Vietnam? Does the conflict in Vietnam threaten the general balance of power, or otherwise justify intervention? Or is it the kind of local conflict, unfortunate for the participants, which the world should pass by on the other side?

From the point of view of the national interests of the United States, there are several answers to the question.

The first is the obligation of the SEATO Treaty. The commitments of that treaty are expressly addressed to the risk which in fact materialized—the risk, that is, that North Vietnam would resume the war.

Secondly, the obligations of the United Nations Charter are not suspended when permanent members of the Security Council disagree. The principles of the Charter are binding on signatories as rules of international law, even though neither the Security Council nor the Assembly has been willing as yet to act officially. Those principles condemn the attack of North Vietnam on South Vietnam, and authorize the members of the organization to offer South Vietnam assistance in its efforts of self-defense.

Thirdly, it has been the judgment of three Presidents and several Congresses that the independence of South Vietnam was directly related to the fate of Southeast Asia as a whole, and therefore to our national interests in a stable balance of power. If South Vietnam were to be forcibly taken over, the parallel expansionist designs of Communist China and North Vietnam would surely be encouraged, and the resistance to these designs seriously weakened throughout the area, and perhaps beyond. Responsible opinion throughout Southeast Asia is agreed that the stakes in Vietnam involve the most drastic alternatives for Southeast Asia and for Asia as a whole. As these lines are written, during the spring of 1968, the pace of guerrilla intrusions in Laos, Thailand, and Burma are increasing, and increasing ominously. The imposition of a Communist government in South Vietnam would menace all hopes of building a strong coalition for peaceful progress in Southeast Asia, and elsewhere as well. It would be a signal for a policy of *sauve qui peut*—and Devil take the hindmost.

Finally, it is obvious that both the Soviet Union and China

regard the conflict in Vietnam as a test for a technique of revolution. As Soviet spokesmen have made clear, nuclear warfare is unthinkable, and massed frontal attacks of the Korean type are too dangerous to be tried. The spread of Communism, they have said, must therefore depend on what they call "wars of national liberation," that is to say, insurrections supported from abroad or the proxy wars which they incite. On their present scale, the hostilities in Vietnam could hardly continue for any length of time without large-scale aid from China and the Soviet Union. De-escalation of the fighting should follow logically if that aid were to be reduced.

So far, however, the Soviet Union has not responded either to proposals of this kind, or to requests that it join with the United Kingdom in reactivating the enforcement procedures for the Geneva agreements dealing with Laos or Vietnam.

Thus the attack on South Vietnam involves the principle of the Truman Doctrine—the challenge we decided to confront in Greece, in Berlin, and in Korea, an attempt to change the boundary between the two systems by force. If this effort prevailed, all that has been gained at such cost in previous tests of the Truman Doctrine would be in doubt. And the instability of the world would increase.

In a fundamental sense, the controversies over the origins of the war in Vietnam are irrelevant. Whether President Eisenhower and the Senate were right or wrong in ratifying the SEATO Treaty; whether President Kennedy made a mistake in beginning to send in large numbers of American troops to enforce that commitment—these issues are of less significance than the dilemma President Johnson has had to confront.

Our presence in South Vietnam has made it possible for the South Vietnamese to create for themselves a constitutional system and the beginnings of national political development, which are by far the most hopeful they have ever had. Most South Vietnamese have committed themselves to this path, and are daily increasing their ability to defend it.

Our commitment to South Vietnam has made it possible for the South Vietnamese to take these steps, steps which offer promise of a truly unified South Vietnam, in which the Vietnamese themselves could make a successful Communist "war of national liberation" an improbability, short of open invasion, such as that of Czechoslovakia. To abandon our commitment at this time would be to undermine this process before it could hope to succeed.

Such an abandonment would be more than a simple act of folly; it would cast a shadow of doubt over the whole network of our security arrangements, the central nervous system of world politics. There would be little security to protect our interests anywhere if America's promise faltered or failed when the going got rough. Such an event would weaken the deterrent influence of our security commitments, which are crucial to the very possibility of world peace.

As President Kennedy once said: "The 1930's taught us a clear lesson: aggressive conduct, if allowed to go unchecked and unchallenged, ultimately leads to war. The nation is opposed to war. We are also true to our word."

If aggression succeeds in South Vietnam it would open a Pandora's box for wars of national liberation, especially in the struggling and disoriented world of the developing countries. If it fails, there is some hope that China will come in time to accept the wisdom of the Truman Doctrine. As President Bourguiba of Tunisia has recently said:

> . . . the problem of Vietnam is not as simple as one thinks. It is a serious problem, involving the equilibrium of the world. . . . An analysis of the events leads to the conclusion that the struggle in Vietnam is taking place between America and China behind the scenes. . . . For Mao Tse-tung the object is to prove that the United States can be brought to capitulation. . . . Things are far from simple, and what is called "imperialism" often is only a matter of opinion. To humanity's misfortune, it happens that peace is founded on the balance of power. . . .

I am not seeking to spare anyone or to please any nation when I say that the world would be in danger the day that, in response to a trend of public opinion, America decided to go back to her former isolationism. . . . China would seize control of all the countries in the region and would wrest leadership of the Communist world from Moscow. And that would be the end of world peace. . . . Hence the conflict we are witnessing has a scope and significance that goes beyond Vietnam.

The continuance of the war, President Bourguiba contends, threatens the modus vivendi on which the chance of peace turns. "One can imagine," he writes, "the mortal danger to which the world would be exposed if East Germany or West Germany were to attempt to achieve, for its own benefit, the unification of the country, as in Vietnam." After each Soviet attempt since the war to extend its sphere of influence, he points out, the Soviets returned to the demarcation line of their sphere of influence. No solution in Vietnam is conceivable without threatening "the balance of the world," President Bourguiba argues, other than the preservation of a South Vietnam free to choose its own course.

Accepting this reasoning, President Johnson has persisted in a course of measured resistance to North Vietnamese aggression, using limited force, and seeking to persuade Moscow, Peking, and Hanoi to live in accordance with the logic of coexistence.

The President has linked the military campaign in Vietnam to three concurrent political campaigns.

The first is addressed to the Soviet Union, and is designed to accomplish two purposes: (1) to reassure the Soviets that our exclusive and limited military goal is to protect South Vietnam, and not to destroy or conquer North Vietnam or to weaken Soviet influence in that country; and (2) to enlist the cooperation of the Soviet Union in persuading the regime in Hanoi to desist from its attempt to unite Vietnam by force. The President accepts the interest of the Soviet Union in helping North Vietnam defend itself. That interest is parallel to our own in the defense of South Vietnam. His concern, in note after note, and in talk after talk, is to invoke the joint responsibility of the two leading powers in the world for the ultimate protection of the peace. The basis of his appeal is the principle of the Truman Doctrine, that in situations like those in Vietnam, Korea, or Germany, the use of force is simply too dangerous to be tolerated.

The President's second diplomatic effort pursues every opportunity to engage the regime in Hanoi in negotiations based on the principles of the Geneva Accords of 1954 and of 1962. In this process, American officials have talked with many representatives of many governments in almost every country of the world, including direct and indirect exchanges with Hanoi.

Three principal lines of approach have been taken by President Johnson.

First, in carrying out his commitment to "unconditional negotiations," we have responded affirmatively to the repeated public appeals of world leaders for peace talks.

Second, we have acted unilaterally on five separate occasions to stop the bombing in order to meet the contention that North Vietnam would move toward peace if we stopped bombing the North.

And, finally, we have approached Hanoi—both directly and through intermediaries—in a serious effort to achieve a settlement or, at least, to bring about reciprocal steps to reduce the level of fighting.

The events of the winter of 1966–1967 illustrate the President's methods in his continuing quest for a peaceful resolution of the Vietnam conflict.

When in December, 1966, efforts through an intermediary to arrange meetings with Hanoi failed, and the bombing pauses over the Christmas and New Year's period resulted only in dramatic increases in infiltration into South Vietnam, direct contacts were established with the North Vietnamese. The substantive exchanges of repeated contacts in January and early February were summarized in messages we conveyed in early February to Chairman Kosygin and Prime Minister Wilson, heads of the Soviet and

British governments, the Co-Chairmen of the Geneva Conference, who were meeting in London.

We informed the British and Soviet representatives that we were ready to stop the bombing of North Vietnam if Hanoi would agree to stop infiltration of the South. In addition, we would also promise not to increase the size of our forces in the South. These assurances could be exchanged secretly, so that the continued suspension of the bombing would appear to be unilateral. We said we should welcome British and Soviet support for this approach.

Although Hanoi had known of this basic position of the United States government for at least three months, on February 8, in an effort to avoid misunderstanding, President Johnson reiterated it in a letter to President Ho Chi Minh, emphasizing that these acts of restraint on both sides would make it possible to conduct serious private discussions leading toward an early peace. Such a meeting, the President stated, could take place in Moscow, Burma, or elsewhere.

Ho Chi Minh's reply on February 15 was harsh and unyielding—halt the bombing "definitely and unconditionally," cease all other acts of war, withdraw all American forces from Vietnam, recognize the Liberation Front as the sole legitimate representatives of the South Vietnamese people, and let the Vietnamese settle their problems themselves. In short, it was a formula for turning South Vietnam over to the Communists and to Hanoi's control.

To slam the door more completely, Hanoi then published President Johnson's letter, though not the communications which had preceded it.

Despite this provocation, President Johnson has refused thus far to publish the documents. His purpose has been to preserve the secrecy of the channel, in the hope that it could someday be used again.

Finally, on March 31, 1968, President Johnson succeeded in obtaining a sign that Hanoi might be ready to discuss the possibility of peace. Our unilateral halt in bombing above the twentieth

71

parallel, coupled with the President's withdrawal from the election of 1968, proved to be a volcanic event, dislodging resistance, at least for a time, to the appearance of negotiation. The result was the start of talks with Hanoi in Paris, and a partial, if temporary, consolidation of national opinion at home.

Our third campaign in Southeast Asia consists in encouraging the non-Communist Asian governments to work together for mutual security and peaceful development. In the Vietnam war itself, there are now more forces sent by our allies than there were in Korea.

Behind the shield of American commitment, the non-Communist governments of Asia have begun to move in new directions. Japan, Australia, New Zealand, Thailand, Malaysia, the Philippines, Singapore, the Republic of Korea, and the Republic of China are evolving toward a broader view of their responsibilities for collective security and development. Indonesia has turned from pro-Communist adventures to a businesslike nationalist government. South Vietnam itself, through five elections in eighteen months, has created a new constitutional base for its national life.

In Asia as in Europe, the Truman Doctrine has encouraged regional forces of cooperation to come into being. Their effect should be felt for many years after the war in Vietnam is brought to a conclusion.

Against this background, it is difficult to translate the furious political arguments of 1967–1968 about our Vietnam policy into words tangible enough to permit analysis. Hostilities in Vietnam, the American people have been told repeatedly on high authority, are an immoral act on the part of the United States, contrary to our national tradition. But those who make such claims never explain why it is immoral for a great power to remain loyal to its treaties, and help a small people resist aggression. The critics protest American bombing, but never elucidate the moral difference between bombing and other forms of warfare, or the indiscriminate terrorism of the Vietcong operations in South Vietnam. Nor do they explain how we could hope to establish conditions of peace in the world without stopping the process of Communist expansion at a given point, and obtaining Soviet and Chinese acceptance of the principle of equilibrium. They never attempt to demonstrate how unilateral withdrawal in Vietnam would affect the credibility of our guarantees elsewhere, or make it politically possible for us to resume the struggle on a more favorable field, short of nuclear war, when aggression against a free country is attempted again, directly or indirectly, with the support of the Soviet Union or China.

The Crisis in the Middle East

The Middle Eastern crisis, lit for a moment in June, 1967, by the lightning flash of the Six-Day War between Israel and her neighbors, has been one of the most serious and difficult problems of recent American foreign policy. The risks before us in the Middle East are unique in one sense—no region of the world, no peoples, and no combination of events can ever be exactly like any others. But the basic processes of world politics which are at work in that region are closely related to those with which we have to deal elsewhere. And the national interests we are defending there—thus far by preventive diplomacy, without military involvement—are comparable to those we are defending also in Europe and the Far East.

Our involvement in the Middle East, like so many other problems we have inherited, is the consequence of the withdrawal of the stabilizing European presence in the area, the weakness, instability, and rivalries of some of the nations of the region, and the fervent ambitions of several schools and sects of revolutionaries, seeking to take advantage of weakness and rivalry in order to advance their own interests.

Throughout the southern part of the Mediterranean basin, the root of trouble is endemic political and social instability. For centuries, the region has not had a coherent and independent political system sustained by its own inherent strength. The proud peoples of the area have been governed by a succession of foreign regimes—Turkish, British, or French. The struggle for independence strengthened national feelings. But the result was not unity or solidarity, but a political fragmentation that discouraged progress and tempted foreign intervention.

The temptation to intervene was reinforced by the fundamental human, economic, and strategic importance of the region. The United States and the nations of Europe have had close and friendly relations with the peoples and governments of the Near and Middle East for generations. The Middle East links three continents. Its air space and waterways are vital to communication between Asia, Europe, and Africa. And they have fundamental strategic importance. The oil resources of the region are of major significance to world commerce. The power to deny access to the Middle East and its resources would be a matter of grave concern to the United States and its allies, in Europe and elsewhere.

In recent years, there have been three main obstacles to achieving conditions of orderly peace in the area. First, there are bitter divisions among the Muslim peoples of the region; secondly, most Arab states regard the establishment of Israel as an injustice to them, and some have insisted on their right to attack its existence; and finally, since 1955, there has been an increasing Soviet presence in the area, as a military, political, and economic influence, and above all as a source of arms.

Many of the divisions among the Muslim peoples of the region have a long history. The long, slow decline of the Ottoman Empire kept many of the peoples of the area under conditions of stagnation, isolated from the modern world. Others, in closer contact with Europe, are at a more advanced stage in education and social development. The drama of Arab liberation during World War I left a legacy of fervent misunderstandings, haphazard boundaries, and disappointed expectations.

The end of European control after the Second World War did little to resolve the divisions among the peoples and governments of the Middle East and North Africa. Traditional rivalries and rivalries of religion are complicated by enmities between monarchists and revolutionaries, and between peoples with differing views about how to organize the process of modernization. As a result, the successor states of the area represent a wide spectrum of political and social forms: there is an extremist revolutionary government in Syria and a traditionalist monarchy in Saudi Arabia. Meanwhile, Iran and Turkey, to the north, and Tunisia, in the west, are becoming vigorous modern communities with close ties to the West. Thus, the Middle East has remained divided, and some parts of the area are in turmoil.

The second factor in this situation, Israel, stands as a tribute to the power of an ideal, the ancient Zionist dream of a return of the Jews from their dispersal. That dream moved toward reality in 1917, when Great Britain issued the Balfour Declaration, promising the Jews a "national home" in Palestine at the end of the war. After the Second World War, the British authorities, hoping to prevent a war between Arab and Jew, struggled in vain to control the flood of European Jews who had survived Hitler. By 1947, the United Nations had accepted the responsibility for Palestine, but the Arabs rejected its partition plan. The result was the new state of Israel, born in a war with the Arabs.

Open war was followed by an inconclusive truce, with many Arab spokesmen professing the view that the establishment of Israel was an injustice that could never be accepted. Several Arab states saw themselves permanently at war with Israel, and claimed the right, at an appropriate moment, to join in a holy war to destroy it.

On the other hand, many other nations, including the United States, have taken a sympathetic interest in the remarkable development of Israel as a progressive and democratic society. They have steadily insisted that while they agree with the Arabs on some important aspects of the Middle Eastern conflict, Israel has the right to live, and no member of the United Nations can claim the right to destroy another.

The increasing Soviet presence in the Middle East has complicated the problem of reaching a stable order, rooted in the region itself, and strong enough to make outside protection unnecessary. In recent years, the Soviet Union has revived the old Russian interest in the Middle East through economic and military aid and close association with the revolutionary parties. In the process, it has become deeply involved in the internal politics of Syria, Egypt, Algeria, and the other states of the area.

Increasingly massive arms shipments to Arab states complemented another Soviet policy in the area, a growing hostility toward Israel. While the Soviet Union had supported the establishment of Israel in 1948, it changed its course during the early 1950's, when it undertook its ambitious campaign to gain influence throughout the area. Hostility to Israel is a policy which much of Arab opinion supports. Many moderate and realistic Arab leaders, eager to get on with tasks of progress, would be happy to end the long period of Arab resistance to the idea of Israel's existence. But, when popular passion on the subject is aroused, they are perforce swept up in the tide. By siding with the Arabs against Israel, and providing them with huge supplies of arms, the Soviet Union gave new impetus to these passionate feelings. At the same time, and as a result, the Western powers could be identified with Israel, which in turn could be depicted as a tool of "Western imperialism." Such a posture would strengthen the radical leaders, parties, and revolutionary groups of the region, who hope to displace moderate regimes oriented to the West.

The intrusion of Soviet influence in the Middle East has given new dimensions to the rivalries and differences among the people of the area. Great Power rivalry in the region exposes many leaders to tensions they find it almost impossible to resolve. And the Soviets' exploitation of the Arab-Israeli conflict, which many Arab leaders would like to forget, requires them to become involved in that tragic and sterile drama against their will.

Given these trends, it is hardly surprising that peace is not the natural state of affairs in the Near East. Its rivalries and counter-rivalries, polarized around the concerns of Great Powers, are formidable obstacles to regional harmony. The process of decolonization led to the British and French intervention in Suez, the protracted war in Algeria, and to wars still in progress in the Arabian peninsula. Among the Arabs, there has been a long history of a continuing covert struggle, resulting from time to time in attempted coups and revolutions, as in Syria and Iraq, or in open civil war and invasion, as in the Yemen. Meanwhile, since the Armistice Agreements of 1949, there has been a smoldering guerrilla war with Israel, a conflict that erupted into full-scale hostilities both in 1956 and in 1967.

By the middle of 1966, it was becoming clear that the situation was heading for another explosion. Organized bands of terrorists, trained in Syria, were entering Israel at an increasing pace, directly from Syria and through Jordan, causing damage, anxiety, and major Israeli retaliation. The issue came before the Security Council twice in the fall of 1966. There was no argument about the facts on either occasion. In the first episode, the government of Syria boasted of its responsibility. But even a mild and ambiguous condemnation of Syria was defeated by a Soviet veto. In the second case, that of the Israeli retaliatory raid against Sam'u in Jordan, Israel was censured.

In the spring of 1967, terrorist penetration of Israel from Syria increased. Rumors were persistently spread that Israel was mobilizing against Syria, although the Secretary General of the United Nations publicly confirmed that these rumors were without foundation. Arab spokesmen began to taunt President Nasser for his inactivity in the face of the supposed threat to Syria. President Nasser responded by moving troops into the Sinai peninsula, and asked the United Nations to remove the forces that had patrolled the border between Israel and Egypt since 1957. In an action which has stirred persistent controversy, the Secretary General responded at once, without going through the consultations his predecessor had indicated he would undertake before withdrawing the troops. The United Nations Emergency Force was suddenly removed, not only from the border, but from the Gaza

Strip and Sharm-al-Sheikh as well. Egyptian troops promptly replaced them, and President Nasser announced that the Strait of Tiran would be closed to Israeli shipping.

At that moment, the situation became one of full crisis. Sharm-al-Sheikh controls access through the Strait of Tiran to the Israeli port of Eilat on the Gulf of Aqaba. Since Egypt has kept the Suez Canal closed to Israeli shipping, in the teeth of two Security Council resolutions, the Strait of Tiran was Israel's only direct opening to Africa and Asia, and its most important source of oil. Closing the strait was in effect an act of blockade.

Egypt's announcement that it would use force to close the strait had another set of consequences. In 1957, we had taken the lead in negotiating the withdrawal of Israeli troops from Sharm-al-Sheikh and the Sinai as a whole, after careful and wide-ranging diplomatic consultations. In 1957, Israel made it clear that if force was used to close the strait, it would regard itself as justified in responding with force, as an act of self-defense authorized under Article 51 of the United Nations Charter. The international understandings of the time were that the Strait of Tiran would be kept open as an international waterway. The United Arab Republic, it is true, never took formal responsibility for this understanding, as it refused to recognize Israel or to deal directly with her. But in every other sense Egypt was a party to and beneficiary of this arrangement, through which Israeli withdrawals had been secured.

As President Johnson remarked later, "If any single act of folly was more responsible for this explosion than any other, I think it was the arbitrary and dangerous announced decision that the Strait of Tiran would be closed."

Throughout this period, President Johnson directed an active diplomatic effort, which had started as a matter of urgency many months before. The goal of our policy was to prevent the outbreak of hostilities and to help deal with the underlying cause of tension in the Middle East.

The President's strategy had several essential elements:

First, all the parties were urged to refrain from using force in any way. And we attempted to mobilize world opinion in behalf of peace. Our views on the nature of the crisis and the dangers of the use of force were communicated to other governments, and made public in a Presidential statement on May 23, 1967. We invited Great Britain, France, and other interested nations to join with us in a concerted diplomatic effort to prevent war, and to make peace.

Secondly, we urgently sought a Security Council resolution calling on the parties to heed the Secretary General's appeal to exercise restraint, forgo belligerence, and avoid all actions which could increase tension. But several key nations refused to take responsibility for a resolution which might have helped to prevent war, by preventing the forcible closing of the Strait of Tiran and the mobilization of Arab armies in a ring around Israel.

Third, we tried to initiate a series of talks with the United Arab Republic in the interest of finding a basis for settlement. The Vice President of that government, Mr. Zachariah Moheiddin, was scheduled to come to Washington on June 7, two days after hostilities broke out.

Meanwhile, as a fourth element in President Johnson's strategy, we and the British proposed to the leading maritime nations a draft declaration reaffirming the view that the Strait of Tiran and the Gulf of Aqaba were international waters, through which innocent passage could not be denied. The maritime nations had taken this position in 1947, and it had been upheld in 1958 in the International Convention on the Law of the Sea. The declaration was to be issued publicly during what turned out to be the week of hostilities.

While these efforts, and others, were being urgently pursued, the situation in the area changed radically. Mobilization and counter-mobilization had replaced the closing of the strait as a threat to the peace. A menacing array of force was approaching the borders of Israel from every side. Jordan put her forces under Egyptian command, and troops from Iraq, Algeria, and Kuwait joined the Egyptians and Syrians. President Nasser openly proclaimed the day of the Holy War.

The air grew dry with menace. The explosion occurred on the morning of June 5.

President Johnson immediately announced the policy we have pursued ever since—to seek an end to hostilities as soon as possible, and at the same time to begin the process of seeking to establish true peace in the area—a condition of peace that could replace the precarious armistice agreements whose inadequacy has been proved so often since 1949.

The United States sought an immediate unconditional cease-fire resolution in the Security Council on the first day of hostilities. The acceptance of this resolution would have kept Jordan from entering the war and prevented the many complications that resulted from its activities. But the Soviets and Arabs did not favor such a proposal. Therefore the Security Council was unable to agree. On Tuesday, June 6, it was at last possible to obtain cease-fire resolutions from the Security Council. Further resolutions, demanding compliance with the earlier call for an end to hostilities, were adopted on June 7 and 9.

The final acceptance of these resolutions, at least by Israel, Egypt, Syria, and Jordan, opened a period of intense discussions, which have yet to reach a conclusion. Despite the continuous efforts of the United States and other governments to get peace negotiations started, it took more than five months to achieve a Security Council resolution, which called on the parties to reach agreement in accordance with certain principles stated in the resolution itself.

These principles follow rather closely those stated by President Johnson in his speech of June 19. That address has been generally recognized as a fair and even-handed statement of the issues, and a proper guide to a just and permanent solution of the Arab-Israeli conflict.

The essential idea of the President's statement is that the continuation of claims of a right to wage war against Israel have become a burden to world peace. It is therefore a world responsibility, and a responsibility of the parties, to achieve an end to such claims—a condition of peace in the area. It should be a fair and dignified peace reached by the parties, not one imposed by conquest, or by the Great Powers. It should recognize each nation's right to live, and to live in security. And it should rest on the principle of the territorial integrity and political independence of all the nations of the area.

On the basis of such a peace, the other principal features of the Arab-Israeli controversy should be resolved by the parties through any procedure on which they can agree. Israeli forces should of course withdraw to agreed and secure boundaries, which should replace the fragile armistice lines of 1948 and 1949. Those armistice agreements expressly contemplated boundary adjustments when they were superseded by arrangements of peace. The tragic problem of the Palestinian refugees should at last be solved. Guarantees should be provided for the use of international waterways by all nations on equal terms. The special interest of three great world religions in the holy places of Jerusalem should be recognized and protected. No unilateral solution of the problem of Jerusalem can be accepted. The international interests in this sacred city are too important to be set aside. Failure to resolve this crucial problem to the general satisfaction could well prevent a lasting settlement in the region. And a start should be made on agreements of arms limitation for the area which could protect the world and the peoples of the region from the risk of another war. The arms race is a tragic waste of resources for any country, but above all for countries with urgent economic problems. Moreover, the constant craving for armaments causes nations to compromise the independence they have fought so fiercely to gain and hold. It makes the whole region a cockpit for the external rivalries of the Great Powers, runs the risk of involving its people in alien quarrels, and postpones indefinitely the region's own genuine self-determination.

The United States has made it unmistakably clear that it is completely opposed to any resumption of hostilities, and that its full support will be given to any procedure which gives promise of fulfilling the principles of the President's statement of June 19.

The effort to translate those principles into a program of negotiation took many months in the Security Council, the General Assembly, and the foreign offices of the entire world. Some of the Arab states and other governments fought tenaciously in the United Nations for a resolution that would seek to restore the situation to what it was on June 4 before any negotiations could begin. As the President remarked on June 19, such a policy "is not a prescription for peace but for renewed hostilities."

On the other hand, the movement from armistice to peace could not condone expansionism. As President Johnson said on June 19, "No nation would be true to the United Nations Charter or to its own true interests if it should permit military success to blind it to the fact that its neighbors have rights and its neighbors have interests of their own. Each nation, therefore, must accept the right of others to live."

The Security Council resolution of November 22, 1967, has been the basis thus far of a protracted and inconclusive series of indirect exchanges through Ambassador Jarring, the Secretary General's representative in seeking to obtain an agreement of the parties through which the resolution could be implemented. The resolution is not self-executing. It is a call for agreement among the parties. But thus far it has not been possible to persuade the parties even to accept the procedure for negotiations in the presence of a United Nations representative, which was successfully used at Rhodes in 1949.

But peace between Israel and its neighbors is only a beginning, though an indispensable beginning, to the task of achieving a stable and progressive order in the area. The bitter heritage of the past will not perish overnight. The risk of war cannot be exorcised until the environment is transformed by fundamental changes in the relations of the states and peoples of the region. Such transformations are occurring in Europe, under the powerful influence of the ideas and arrangements of the European Community. Similar efforts have been launched in other areas of the world—in Central America and in Southeast Asia, for example.

Like efforts are needed to help the peoples of the Middle East adapt their societies and economies to the level of their aspirations. The Arabs of the area must themselves find the means to restore the fertile gardens of their past. In such an area effort they could have no better partners than the Israelis, their ancient cousins, who have struggled for centuries to preserve their culture and adapt it to the task of modern life. What a tragedy it would be if the opportunity for so fruitful a partnership should be lost in fratricide.

Our government has devoted unremitting efforts to the search for peace in the Middle East. As President Johnson said on June 19, 1967:

> If the nations of the Middle East will turn toward the works of peace, they can count with confidence upon the friendship and the help of all the people of the United States of America.
>
> In a climate of peace we here will do our full share to help with a solution for the refugees. We here will do our full share in support of regional cooperation. We here will do our share— and do more—to see that the peaceful promise of nuclear energy is applied to the critical problem of desalting water. . . .

But success in such efforts to achieve regional cooperation can hardly be taken for granted. It will not be easy for the Middle East to become a stable and progressive region, open to the world but free from outside interference.

Success in that effort cannot be imposed from without, either by the United States or by anyone else. We and other friendly nations can discourage the coercive designs of others, and encourage promising forces and initiatives originating within the region. The Great Powers can prevent success, although they cannot guarantee it. They cannot do for the region what its own people refuse to do. But they can help those people in productive partnership if they themselves pursue the road to peace.

CHAPTER 6

Concert and Conciliation: The Task of Building a New World Order

THE DRAMA of crisis situations is hardly the whole of American foreign policy. Minimal public order in the world is not the end of our foreign policy, but its precondition. Beyond the effort to prevent a slide toward chaos, programs are pursued day by day to strengthen cooperation in developing the Free World and to improve political relations with the states governed by Communist parties. Concert among the free nations and conciliation with the Communists—these have been the major thrusts of American policy in this period. They can be seen at work in many contexts —in the diplomacy of our direct relations with the Soviet Union and Communist China; in our initiatives to strengthen NATO and the Atlantic Community, to support the European movement, and to deepen our relations with Canada, Japan, and many other countries; in our bilateral and multilateral aid programs; in negotiations with respect to disarmament, the peaceful uses of outer space, and nuclear control; and in many projects to fortify an open and progressive world economy.

The Relationship with the Soviet Union

A central concern of American policy has been and will necessarily continue to be the relationship between the United States and the Soviet Union, the most dangerous and most promising of all the "special" relationships which exist between the United States and other countries. President Johnson has been the boldest and most persistent of our recent Presidents in seeking to improve relations with the Soviet Union. His purpose is ambitious: to transform the relationship between the two countries into one of cooperation, rather than of suspicious rivalry.

On August 26, 1966, in Arco, Idaho, President Johnson said:

. . . At the heart of our concern in the years ahead must be our relationship with the Soviet Union. Both of us possess unimaginable power; our responsibility to the world is heavier than that ever borne by any two nations at any other time in history. Our common interests demand that both of us exercise it wisely in the years ahead.

Since 1945, we have opposed Communist efforts to bring about a Communist-dominated world. We did so because our convictions and our interests demanded it; and we shall continue to do so.

But we have never sought war or the destruction of the Soviet Union; indeed, we have sought instead to increase our knowledge and our understanding of the Russian people with whom we share a common feeling for life, a love of song and story, and a sense of the land's vast promises.

Our compelling task is this: to search for every possible area of agreement that might conceivably enlarge, no matter how slightly or how slowly, the prospect for cooperation between the United States and the Soviet Union. In the benefits of such cooperation, the whole world would share and so, I think, would both nations.

The Soviet Union is a dimension, and often the decisive

dimension of many of our policies—those in Vietnam and the Middle East, our NATO policy, and many, many others as well. One can see the positive side of our effort to improve relations with the Soviet Union in the history of a number of recent projects.

The United States has patiently sought agreement with the Soviet Union, and with other nations, on a treaty to end the risk that nuclear weapons spread throughout the world. Under such a treaty, the nuclear powers which sign would undertake not to transfer such weapons to other states, nor help them build nuclear weapons. At the same time, the signatories which do not possess nuclear weapons would promise not to become nuclear weapons powers.

Manifestly, the project has significant implications for peace. It could rest only on Soviet-American agreement with respect to a subject of fundamental importance to both nations, and to the world. The fact of that agreement should be a cohesive political force, tending to prevent serious division on lesser problems. It would make the world political system more manageable, and reduce the risk of nuclear war, and indeed of any general war.

But the proposed treaty bristles with difficulties, both real and psychological. Some non-nuclear states feel that signing the treaty would imply their permanent acceptance of second-class political status. All are concerned about the possibilities of nuclear blackmail by or through some of the nuclear states. The industrial states wish to be certain that signing the treaty would not inhibit their progress in the peaceful uses of nuclear energy and technology. And the United States has been particularly concerned to make certain that the treaty not stand in the way of the process of European unification, weaken the Atlantic Alliance, or constitute a strain in our relations with Japan, India, or any other state.

Years of effort have gone into the Non-Proliferation Treaty. These explorations reached a decisive stage in the fall of 1966, when the United States concluded, on the basis of several crucial talks with the Soviet Union, that agreement on a treaty was possible. At that point, we suspended our talks with the Soviet Union in order to engage in consultations with our European allies, and with other states to which we are closely bound. Those talks were successfully conducted during 1966 and 1967, both bilaterally and through the North Atlantic Council, the consultative body on the North Atlantic Alliance.

As these pages are written, in the summer of 1968, the treaty has been signed by the United States, the Soviet Union, Great Britain, and some seventy other governments. The process of ratification is under way.

The fate of the treaty is by no means certain, however, for political explosions—in Central Europe or elsewhere—could still prevent the treaty from becoming fully effective.

But in this major area diplomacy has removed many formidable barriers, reinforced mutual understanding between the United States and its allies, and added another positive strand to the relationship between the United States and the Soviet Union.

Progress toward cooperation with the Soviet Union is slow. Indeed, it is difficult to be sure that real progress has in fact occurred. Many of our offers of cooperation—in exploring outer space, for example, in controlling ballistic missiles and anti-ballistic missiles, and in satellite communication—have so far been unanswered. But they are renewed, in the hope that someday the Soviet leaders will accept the full alternative of peaceful cooperation with us.

Despite the strain for us arising from Soviet behavior in Vietnam and the Middle East, President Johnson has sought to persuade Congress to remove legal obstacles to trade with Eastern Europe and the Soviet Union, and to broaden the contacts among our peoples in the fields of education, cultural exchange, and tourism. We have recently ratified a consular agreement with the Soviet Union, and a civil aviation agreement. Both should enlarge the area of peaceful contact among the peoples of the two countries. And in 1967 we completed the ratification of the Treaty on the Peaceful Use of Outer Space, a major achievement, banning both national sovereignty and war from this new frontier of mankind.

The Soviet invasion of Czechoslovakia in 1968 has raised basic questions about the aims and orientation of Soviet policy. As these pages are written, it is too soon to be sure whether their move was a panicky defensive step, or the prelude to another round of the Cold War. All that is clear is that it will make projects of cooperation more difficult to carry through on both sides.

There are peaks and troughs in the pattern of our relation with the Soviet Union. When progress occurs, we have a tendency to euphoria. When there is a setback, some of us are inclined to think that the end of the world is about to take place. But beyond moods and illusions the realities survive—realities of interest and of opportunity.

There is nothing inevitable about foreign policy. The history of this century is a catalogue of catastrophes that could have been prevented by wiser and more energetic officials. But if anything is predictable in this field, it is that the Soviet Union and the United States will continue to grope toward an understanding, because both know how much is at stake.

Communist China

It is too soon to measure the chances of success in our attempts at achieving better relations with the Soviet Union. Appeals to Communist China are obviously addressed to an even more remote future. But they are made, and repeated. In his State of the Union message of January 10, 1967, President Johnson said:

> We shall continue to hope for a reconciliation between the people of mainland China and the world community. . . . We should be the first to welcome a China which decided to respect her neighbor's rights. We would be the first to applaud her were she to apply her great energies and intelligence to improving the welfare of her people. And we have no intention of

trying to deny her legitimate needs for security and friendly relations with her neighboring countries.

During the 1966 debate over seating Communist China in the United Nations, there was a significant change in the position of the United States. Instead of flatly opposing Communist China's entry, we supported a resolution calling for the appointment of a study committee to examine the complex problem that would be involved in considering the possibility of Chinese Communist membership. The resolution was defeated in 1966, and again in 1967. But it will probably be presented again under more favorable circumstances.

The future of China, and its future orientation, are among the most fundamental topics of world politics. The foreign policy of the United States takes them deeply into account in its planning, and in its dispositions.

The Atlantic Alliance

Like his three immediate predecessors, President Johnson views the Atlantic Alliance as a first principle of our foreign policy.

In an address on October 7, 1966, he said: "Americans and all Europeans share a connection which transcends political differences. We are a single civilization; we share a common destiny; our future is a common challenge."

Turning to the Alliance, he said: "The bonds between the United States and its Atlantic partners provide the strength on which the world's security depends. Our interdependence is complete"—in security, in economic affairs, in science and technology, in our relations with the developing nations, and in planning and carrying out political initiatives to heal the divisions of Europe. "Our first concern," he went on, "is to keep NATO strong and abreast of the times. . . . The Atlantic Alliance is a living organization. It must adapt to changing conditions." The President called for "a new thrust for the Alliance." "We know," he said, "that the world is changing. Our policy must reflect the reality of today—not yesterday. In every part of the world, new forces are at the gates: new countries, new aspirations, new men."

In this connection, I propose to challenge one of the most familiar clichés in the voluminous literature, journalism, and rhetoric of our foreign policy. It is conventional wisdom, repeated everywhere as commonplace, that we have no European and Atlantic policy, that NATO is in disarray, and that we have been neglecting our vital interests in Europe because we have been so preoccupied with Asia, or so eager to reach an agreement with the Soviet Union.

I submit that these propositions constitute a myth, that here, as elsewhere, there is a notable gap—perhaps even a credibility gap—between cliché and reality in the vocabulary of common opinion.

The relationship between the United States and Europe is rich in the complexity of deep and intimate human ties. We share a common civilization, common values, a common personal heritage. The European bond is an insistent element in almost every aspect of all our lives. Generations of novelists, historians, and scholars have explored it but failed to capture its final mystery. I shall confine myself to the more mundane aspects of our relationship. But all our ties are colored by the nature of their matrix.

Like every other feature of our foreign policy, our relations with Europe are in motion, and often in turbulent motion, as we and the nations of Europe seek to reshape the pattern of our cooperation in the light of changing world conditions. But the fact of that cooperation remains a premise of our foreign policy, and of Europe's, for the most fundamental reasons of shared interest. The principle of close cooperation between the United States and Europe, and Japan as well—the main power centers of the Free World—has been basic to our foreign policy for at least twenty years. It is indispensable to the quest for world equilibrium which has engaged four administrations since the war. And it will necessarily remain central to our national policy in the struggle for peace for as far ahead as we can foresee.

The cooperation of Europe and the United States is fruitful and constructive. Month after month, it results in agreed solutions for difficult problems in many fields: in the military area, of course; in trade; in monetary affairs; in programs of aid for the developing countries; in the field of disarmament and arms limitation; in the handling of thorny political troubles in many parts of the world; in INTELSAT, the instrument for international cooperation in space satellite communications; in the development of initiatives to improve our relations with the Communist countries; and most recently in the articulation by NATO, in December, 1967, of a program to give new vitality and new dimensions to the political work of the Atlantic Alliance.

I do not wish to minimize the disagreements we have had with one or another of our European partners from time to time, nor to pretend that they do not exist. I do wish, however, to put those disagreements into the perspective of an overall record of solid progress in many fields during the last few years.

Europe has of course fully recovered from the war and from the shock of decolonization. But European societies are more fragile than they were, and less confident, after the storms and strains of this violent century. And Europe has not emotionally accepted the changed contours of this century, any more than we have.

The reversal of roles between Europe and the United States since the war is a source of strain on both sides of the Atlantic. Europe does not enjoy the loss of primacy. And we resent, indeed, we can hardly bring ourselves to recognize, the circumstances which have required us to assume that responsibility. For both peoples, the course of policy since 1945 is profoundly at variance with their sense of the past.

Both Europe and the United States realize that the great tasks of the next generation, from the reconciliation of Europe to the achievement of order and progress in the third world, can be accomplished only if the Atlantic nations and Japan concert their policies. On the other hand, both Europe and the United States confront strong and reciprocal political impulses favoring withdrawal and isolation.

The best cure for these strains is the experience of confronting one problem after another, and finding cooperative solutions for them. That has been President Johnson's purpose in seeking a new start for the Atlantic Community, particularly in the political work of the Alliance, and in the programs of the OECD.

One goal in the development of the Atlantic Alliance has been to help Europe achieve a new coherence and a new stability within a steadily more coherent and effective Atlantic Community—a community, that is, viewed not only as a set of formal committees, but as a network of cooperative habits and intimacies. Our aim has never been an "American" Europe—an Atlantic empire which would result in American hegemony. The notion of empire is repugnant to the most fundamental tenets of our policy. We shall always prefer patterns of cooperation to Roman solutions. From the beginning we have sought not only to restore and preserve Western Europe's independence but to foster conditions which would make it possible for our European allies to resume that full place in the world which their talent, wealth, and experience entitle—indeed, oblige—them to hold. With the Marshall Plan, we sought to build not an economic dependency but a powerful competitor. No one needs to be reminded how well our hopes have been fulfilled.

Most of the credit for Europe's revival belongs, obviously, to the Europeans themselves. Their history since the war exhibits not only the characteristic vitality of these ancient and inexhaustible nations but their political maturity and institutional inventiveness as well.

Perhaps the greatest achievement of postwar European statesmanship has been the articulation and acceptance of the European idea, which has made possible the fundamental reconciliation between France and Germany. It ranks, I believe, with the Marshall Plan as one of the truly creative acts of modern politics. It has liberated the energies that have made possible the achievements of the European communities and started a process of evolution which, despite all obstacles, is still gaining in momentum.

In short, it is fair to say that Western Europe, more than any other region of the world, has made progress in reconciling the fact of nationalism to the fact of interdependence.

The same recognition of interdependence has extended not only among the Europeans but across the Atlantic. For nearly twenty years we and our allies have cooperated intimately in sustaining Western Europe's military defense, as well as in business, economic policy, education, and science.

The Atlantic link has meant that in a turbulent world Europe has already enjoyed a period of peace longer than that between the First and Second World Wars.

But Europe does not enjoy real peace. Its present order is not generally accepted as right by the European peoples themselves. For Europe is not just Western Europe, but Eastern Europe as well. Germany is not two nations, but one. There cannot be a true détente in Europe until the wound that runs across its face is healed. It is equally apparent that the reunification of Germany and of Europe can be achieved only by détente, that is, only through improvements in the political climate of Europe and of the world at large. The stability of NATO and the economic and social progress of Western Europe have helped to release humanistic influences in Eastern Europe; thus they provide the foundation for new initiatives to improve political and economic relations with the countries of Eastern Europe. They also generate fears in the suspicious minds of Russian conservatives that progress toward liberty and a reduction of tensions would end Communist control in Eastern Europe, and perhaps in the Soviet Union as well.

Until the summer of 1968, the long period of peace and the evident popular feeling on both sides of the ideological boundary had raised hopes that some reconciliation of the European family might be possible before too long.

The Federal Republic of Germany had embarked upon an

Eastern policy designed to rebuild its ties of trade and culture, and its political relationships to Eastern Europe. If such a policy offers little prospect for the immediate reunification of Germany, it could prepare the way by altering the atmosphere and breaking down the sense of sullen isolation that breeds unreasonable fears. Eventually, in a changed climate, it should not be beyond the realm of possibility that the same inventiveness which has been devoted to building the new environment of Western Europe and of the Atlantic Community could find a formula to end artificial barriers that can only be sustained by force.

Similarly, we have supported another important plank in the foreign policy of the German government: that of close collaboration between Germany and France. We have encouraged Franco-German reconciliation since the war as the indispensable basis for the formation of Europe. We continue to believe that the stability of Europe and of the world requires not only an erosion of the barriers between East and West but a strong Western grouping to provide a reasonable counterpoise to the immense bulk of Russia. Such a Western grouping is the best possible basis for stable cooperation with the Soviet Union and Eastern Europe, and for the full participation of Western Europe as our equal partner in all the works of peace.

The United States has continued to believe that a genuinely stable West European grouping, whatever form it may ultimately take, requires the presence of Britain. Both President Kennedy and President Johnson have expressed regret at the circumstances which have thus far prevented Britain and other applicants from becoming members of the European communities. That delay has in turn delayed the evolution of a political Europe and perhaps also of a European defense community.

The ultimate shape and character of Europe are for Europeans to decide. But the whole Free World has a natural interest in the success of a movement which could contribute so much to its capacity for order and for progress.

A stable settlement for Europe requires more than a closely

knit Western Europe strong enough to conduct healthy relations with the East. It requires also a vital and modern Atlantic Alliance and the dynamic development of the Atlantic Community.

The interdependence of the United States and Europe is now more complete than it was twenty years ago. The implacable logic of the nuclear deterrent constitutes one dimension of that interdependence. In this field, Europe and the United States will have to remain together indefinitely. The progressive integration of the European and American economies, university systems, and institutions of research constitutes another.

The moral of recent experience in the field of trade and monetary affairs is that the economies of Europe, the United States, Canada, and Japan are now so large and have such deep interconnections that they simply must be planned and managed together. If one large unit gets out of phase with the others, the result is disequilibrium in the system as a whole.

It is equally clear that collaboration in science and technology, both in business and in academic institutions, is the quickest way to overcome technological gaps in either direction across the Atlantic and the Pacific.

Universities have always been an international fraternity of scholars, at one remove from the political power. In the long run their integrity and their creativity depend equally upon their freedom. If knowledge is to develop fully as a common resource, it is vital that the institutions of knowledge be kept open to all comers of talent. In this sphere, parochialism is self-defeating. No one can know in advance where the next breakthrough will originate.

These immense forces bind the Atlantic community together: the nuclear imperative and the equally compelling imperatives of economics, science, technology, and knowledge generally. They supplement the community's human and cultural bonds and give urgency to its political development. In these areas, there are simply no real alternatives to Atlantic cooperation if Europe and the United States continue to respect their vital national interests in the making of foreign policy, and indeed of policy in many other realms.

But continuity of interests need not and should not imply a continuity of institutional forms. The patterns of Atlantic cooperation that were designed in the late forties and the early fifties are not necessarily appropriate today. In that era, Europe was slowly recovering from the war and enduring the final stages of decolonization. Today, Europe has completed its spectacular recovery, while the United States continues to bear a heavy share of the Free World's common defense burden. Isolationist and illusionary policies in Europe reinforce those on this side of the Atlantic.

Obviously, in the face of that risk, the course of wisdom is not a general American withdrawal, which would invite chaos and war, but a more rapid rallying of our allies, both Atlantic and Pacific, to join us as equals in the vital tasks of peace-keeping and aid.

American public opinion will always support a full American quota of collective responsibility, so long as that effort is reciprocated by our allies. On the other hand, irresponsibility on one side of the Atlantic breeds irresponsibility on the other. I do not believe that the United States will repeat its folly of 1920—that of repudiating President Wilson and seeking refuge in the isolationism of the nineteenth century. But the risk is there. And now—as always in our history—there are strong voices in praise of such a course.

Allied cooperation is the best vaccination against that risk.

In October, 1966, President Johnson proposed a program of action to modernize the Alliance. The Alliance, he said, must become a forum for increasingly close consultations. These should cover the full range of joint concerns—from East-West relations to crisis management.

In the spirit of these words, the United States has worked with its allies in recent years to find cooperative solutions for many of the principal problems confronting us. Consultation between the Atlantic nations and Japan was the predicate for the success of the Kennedy Round of tariff negotiations and for the Rio agreement and other acts of cooperation in the field of monetary policy—policies which strengthen the open, liberal, and progressive economy of the Free World.

Similar procedures of consultation resolved difficult problems in the development of the draft treaty to prevent the proliferation of nuclear weapons, and in reaching agreements on allied force levels in Europe. The United States, Europe, and Japan are now full partners in the many-sided enterprise of providing economic assistance to the developing countries.

Above all, the last year witnessed the successful start of a project to give the North Atlantic Alliance major political responsibilities. The allies conducted a year-long study of the future political tasks of the Alliance as an influence for a durable peace in the world.

The Alliance regrouped effectively in the wake of France's decision in 1966 to withdraw from the military organization of NATO. The other fourteen allies decided to maintain the integrated system of military defense which had proved so effective since 1949. Both the military and the political arms of NATO were transferred to Brussels. And both have been actively developed and reformed in the process.

On the military side, two new bodies have been organized for allied consultations on nuclear problems. A new system of NATO satellite communications is being prepared. And dangerous pressures to reduce NATO's military strength for financial reasons have been met by agreements among Britain, Germany, and the United States. Those agreements call for the allies to deal with the foreign exchange consequences of the allied troop presence in Germany not by offsetting military purchases alone, but by cooperation in the management of monetary reserves, and other forms of financial cooperation as well.

In December, 1967, the foreign ministers of the Atlantic Alliance agreed that, while the growing military strength of the Soviet

Union and the enigmatic course of its policies did not in all prudence permit a unilateral reduction of allied force levels in Europe and the Mediterranean, the political aspects of the work of the Alliance should take on a new dimension, and a new importance. As a defensive alliance, NATO has always had political responsibilities. Its purpose is not only to deter aggression, but to provide the foundation for policies directed at achieving détente. The relative stability of East-West relations since 1962 and other changes in the international situation permitted the allies to take the initiative in proposing policies designed to improve political relations with the Communist countries, and to achieve balanced and mutual force reductions. In order to carry forward its political initiatives, the ministers decided to deepen and improve the practice of consultation within the Alliance.

These decisions should prove to be a political catalyst for the Alliance. The ministers directed the North Atlantic Council to start its new political course by undertaking studies and developing plans for action with respect to a number of crucial problems—particularly European security, including the German problem; arms control and disarmament; and the security of the Mediterranean flank of Europe. And they instructed the Council to turn its attention beyond the limits of the treaty area. The security of the Alliance, they said, "cannot be treated in isolation from the rest of the world. Crises and conflicts arising outside the area may impair its security either directly or by affecting the global balance." In carrying out this responsibility, the Council may use working groups consisting of those allies who wish to engage in such studies—an important principle, which should make the Alliance a more flexible and effective instrument for harmonizing allied diplomatic policy on a number of fundamental problems —those of the Middle East and Africa, for example.

With respect to the critically important problem of Germany, the Alliance recorded its agreement with the thesis President Johnson advanced in his speech of October 7, 1966: that there could be no genuine détente in Europe until the German problem is solved, and no solution of the German problem without a détente, that is, without a genuine improvement in political relations with the countries of Eastern Europe.

On the basis of this study, the allies concluded that it would be imprudent to reduce Western military strength and capability to deter aggression unless the Soviet government undertook also to reduce the strength of the Soviet and Warsaw Pact forces in Eastern Europe, and of Soviet forces in the Atlantic and the Mediterranean. One-sided reductions of Western strength would remove any incentive for force reductions on the Soviet side and increase both the military and the political risks on the flanks of Europe and in Europe itself. It would tend to weaken or eliminate non-nuclear options in the event of renewed turbulence over Berlin or other trouble spots in or near Europe. And under present circumstances it would give rise to serious risks of miscalculation.

Changes in troop disposition are volcanic political events, as we have learned to our cost over and over again, from Greece to Korea. A unilateral cut in NATO forces could have the most profound and most negative aspect on both sides of the ideological boundary in Europe.

In a report made public in December, 1967, the allies therefore concluded:

> . . . one of the foundations for achieving an improvement in East/West relations and a peaceful settlement in Europe must be NATO's continuing military strength and capability to deter aggression. In this connection they noted that the Soviet Union continues to expend increasing resources upon its powerful military forces and is developing types of forces designed to enable it to achieve a significant military presence in other parts of the world. They also observed that during the past year there has been a marked expansion in Soviet forces in the Mediterranean. . . .
>
> Military security and a policy of détente are not contradictory but complementary. Collective defence is a stabilizing factor in world politics. It is the necessary condition for effective

100

policies directed towards a greater relaxation of tensions. The way to peace and stability in Europe rests in particular on the use of the Alliance constructively in the interest of détente.

The need for agreed and stable force levels in Europe at this time does not, of course, mean that NATO is forever frozen in its present posture. As a defensive alliance, NATO's purpose is basically political: to permit us through diplomacy to seek an end of the danger which called NATO into being twenty years ago.

At the June, 1968, meeting of the foreign ministers of NATO, a bold proposal was made to the Soviet Union and the countries of Eastern Europe to join NATO in seeking agreed ways to reduce force levels in Europe and to achieve agreements of arms limitation. Such proposals could profoundly reduce the level of tension in Europe, and pave the way for new European security arrangements which could open the door to détente.

The course indicated by NATO's 1968 Reykjavik proposals points the way to the only possible resolution of the problem of European security. The police methods of the Stalinist era cannot for long contain or control the societies of Eastern Europe. Only a general relaxation of tensions could permit the peaceful evolution of Europe without risk of explosion.

Strengthening the Economy of the Free World

For the Johnson Administration, one of its most critical and successful concerns has been the consolidation of the new international economy that American policy has fostered since 1945. To understand our policy over the past few years, we must go back to the end of the war and the beginning of the long, patient, and, on the whole, successful effort to construct a new order out of the ashes of the old system which the war had finally destroyed.

In 1945 we had most of the world's monetary reserves. Ours was the only economy in the Free World which had not been gravely damaged or weakened.

101

The nations of Western Europe and Japan, on the other hand, had been badly hurt, and starved for capital. And the emerging nations of Asia and Africa were just beginning their hazardous efforts to gain control of their own destinies.

Even before the war was over, we made offers of reconstruction loans under the Lend-Lease Act, both to the Soviet Union and to our allies in Western Europe. The Soviet Union declined the offer. But our first assistance to the reconstruction of Europe began as early as February, 1945. The Marshall Plan, Point Four, and many other programs of economic aid and development followed.

These programs have been strikingly successful. They have encouraged the mobilization of enterprise and of capital throughout the world. Europe and Japan were restored, and have bounded forward. Currencies became convertible. Starting with the impulse of the Marshall Plan, and its call for European cooperation, the Europe of the Six was formed, a step of profound political as well as economic significance. Restrictions on capital transfers were gradually removed. With ingenuity, imagination, and good will, the central bankers learned how to cooperate successfully. They helped to forge a monetary system capable of assuring the entire Free World both full employment and growth, with a minimum of inflation. And, step by step, year by year, negotiation by negotiation—from the Dillon Round to the Kennedy Round—restrictions on trade were dismantled, to permit all nations to benefit from the economies of comparative advantage, and to enjoy the fruits of a more rational division of labor.

This process rested on three related sets of principles—those of the Bretton Woods agreements in the field of monetary policy; those of GATT in trade policy; and those of aid in our common commitment to assist the development of the countries of the Southern Hemisphere. Liberal trade, liberal investment policy, a unitary and progressive monetary system, and programs of aid—these have been the pillars of our economic policy since the war. Success in any one realm depended upon success in the others.

The relatively open and efficient world economy of the sixties is not a construct only of trade policy, or of monetary policy, or of investment and aid policy, but of all three. These related and mutually reinforcing policies could prevail only through building habits of effective and confident cooperation among all the countries concerned, often through new international institutions—GATT, the European Communities, EFTA, the IMF and the World Bank, and OECD.

The political significance of these developments is apparent. With the protection of allied security arrangements backed by the deterrent power of the United States, the Free World has moved along the road toward rapid economic progress through methods which have intensified cohesion, and interposed a powerful barrier to centrifugal and divisive forces. We are becoming a single Free World economy, not a weak agglomeration of rival blocs.

The fuel for this process of economic integration and growth has been America's capacity and willingness to run balance-of-payments deficits—our willingness, that is, to export more capital every year than our current surplus on trade account—and to finance these deficits through the systematic reduction of gold reserves. This policy permitted the creation of a solid foundation for the cooperative monetary system we know today. And the large-scale exports of American capital and management have proved to be catalysts of progress everywhere.

However helpful our balance-of-payments deficits have been in financing the reconstruction and the rapid development of a unified Free World economy, based on liberal principles of trade and finance, they could not go on forever. Some years ago, perceptive men on both sides of both oceans began to prepare cooperative programs for achieving equilibrium in the world's balance of payments against the day when American deficits were ended—an equilibrium that could permit free movements of trade and of capital to continue, and could equally finance the indispensable security needs of the Free World.

103

These steps have involved both unilateral and cooperative steps.

On the American side, starting in the early sixties, we took a series of measures to offset and reduce our balance-of-payments deficits. Later, we instituted voluntary programs to limit our export of capital, in order to help confine the total outflow of dollars to roughly the amount of foreign currencies earned every year by the American economy, less our foreign-exchange expenditure for security and tourism.

Through these arrangements—the offset agreements with respect to our military positions abroad, and the voluntary programs of capital export restraint—we began to reduce our deficits. Within recent years—until the last quarter of 1967, in fact—they were running at the comparatively low level of $1.5 to $2 billion a year.

At the same time, the countries of the West began to coordinate their economic policies more closely. The European and American economies bulk so large nowadays in world economic affairs that they have to remain in phase. If either Europe or the United States expands when it should contract, or contracts when it should expand, flows of trade and of capital are immediately affected, and balance-of-payments disequilibrium emerges. At an earlier stage of postwar economic history, such a disequilibrium was not of primary importance. For the last few years, it has become critical.

The decline in the volume of American deficits created another and equally fundamental problem: a prospective shortage of reserves. The American deficits had been used by the world monetary system for a long time as a factor nearly equivalent to one of the great discoveries of gold in the past. Dollars were used to settle international transactions, and were held as reserves. This fact did not represent a conscious decision on our part. It simply reflects the convenience and versatility of the New York financial market as an attractive place to hold funds in liquid form.

At about the same time that American deficits began to diminish, newly mined gold ceased to be available to the world monetary system on a significant scale. The industrial demand for gold increased. In recent years, the speculative demand for gold became important, and finally, during the latter part of 1967 and the early months of 1968, decisive.

Starting in 1965, the world's monetary authorities began to work on plans to prepare the monetary system for the end of American deficits, and the manifest inadequacy of gold production. The Secretary of the Treasury, Henry H. Fowler, has played a notable role in this effort, which has required years of creative study and negotiation. It reached its climax in September, 1967, in the agreement on the Special Drawing Rights Plan for the International Monetary Fund, which was approved by the Congress in 1968.

The Special Drawing Rights plan represents a major improvement in the organization of the world monetary system—the most important reform since the Bretton Woods Conference in 1944. It should give the International Monetary Fund some of the indispensable flexibility in monetary management the Federal Reserve System has within the United States. The plan will permit the nations represented in the fund to establish a special form of credit, which can be used by central banks as a reserve. The creation and use of the new credits will be under the control of the international monetary authorities, acting together in the interest of avoiding either depression or inflation. The availability of these credits will not solve the balance-of-payments problems of a particular country, or make internal discipline less fundamental as an international obligation of each important trading country. But they should protect all countries against the pressures of a general shortage of reserves. Such shortages would impose strains on the monetary system as the era of dollar deficits comes to an end. They could lead many countries to limit trade, capital movements and tourism, in an effort to protect their international position by restrictive measures.

It was permissible in the summer and fall of 1967 to think that we had made adequate preparations for the era of equilibrium, and that the economic system we and other nations had been working so hard to establish had been consolidated. The Kennedy Round agreements had been reached in the early summer. The SDR plan was approved by the delegates to the Rio de Janeiro conference in September, 1967. The horizon looked clear, and the outlook sunny. We faced no real risks, many thought, apart from the problem of curbing the boom in our own economy, and taking certain other steps to reduce our balance-of-payments deficit.

However, 1967 and 1968 have proved to be years in which it was always prudent to expect the unexpected. The end of 1967 saw a dangerous monetary explosion, which could have wrecked the Free World economy, and undone all that had been achieved by twenty years of enlightened international economic cooperation.

The crisis measured the impact of two fundamental factors on confidence: the delay in the passage of American tax surcharge legislation, which President Johnson recommended earlier in 1967, and the devaluation of the pound.

The delay in the passage of our tax legislation meant that our boom proceeded at an excessive rate. When the American economy is booming, its appetite for imports rises, and rises very rapidly. At the same time, the outflow of capital from the United States continued at a high level. And American tourists continued to show great enthusiasm for foreign travel. Of the balance-of-payments deficit of $3.6 billion in 1967, more than half was attributable to the fact that our citizens spent abroad $2 billion more than foreign travelers spent in the United States. The expenses of the war in Vietnam added another $1.5 billion to the deficit.

In the third quarter of 1967, the deficit was running at the annual level of $2.5 billion, slightly above estimates. But the situation was transformed by the devaluation of sterling in November. That proved to be a volcano in the world monetary system, generating fears that a change in the dollar price of gold was inevitable. These fears were translated into a virulent attack of gold fever, which led to large-scale movements of capital both from London and from New York.

On the first day of 1968, the United States announced a drastic program to help bring the world balance of payments into equilibrium. We imposed severe curbs on the outflow of funds. And we initiated a series of consultations with the chief trading nations of the world, seeking agreement on a number of steps we could take, separately and together, to move world trade and finance toward equilibrium. President Johnson's goal was to achieve equilibrium through procedures of international cooperation, rather than by unilateral action, and to do so in ways which expanded trade and did not restrict it.

The guidelines for this sequence of moves were laid down in the 1966 report of the OECD on the Balance of Payments Adjustment Process, which all the members of that organization have accepted. That report recognizes the necessity for the coordination of economic policy both by surplus countries and deficit countries in the common interest of equilibrium.

In recent years, our balance-of-payments deficit has corresponded to a European surplus. Both Europe and the United States have been working together vigorously to restore equilibrium. We have reduced our capital exports. Europe has increased hers. Our interest rates have gone up. Europe has sought to keep hers lower. We have sought to dampen our boom. Europe has been speeding up her rate of internal growth—a process which increases her imports and tends to reduce her exports. A study was begun in GATT to examine the trade consequences of border taxes and other nontariff barriers, with a view to preparing an equitable long-run solution for these vexing trade problems. And, finally, the chief trading nations of the world—the European Community, the EFTA countries, Canada, and Japan joined in a proposal to accelerate their Kennedy Round cuts unilaterally, and allow us to decelerate ours, in the interest of helping to improve our trade surplus and to make it unnecessary for us to consider any special measures of trade restriction in order to reach balance-of-payments equilibrium. At the time of writing, many of these initiatives are still in train, and new elements—the French disruptions of May and June, 1968, for example—have intervened to change the situation in ways that will take time to become clear.

Whatever the outcome of particular initiatives, the pattern of collective action in this crisis has significance in itself, both politically and economically. It reflects a habit of solidarity in the common interest of economic growth.

The monetary authorities also have been working together with imagination. Confronting a speculative fever that threatened to get out of hand, they took basic steps that should liberate the monetary system from speculative influences and make its cooperative management more feasible than ever.

Some of the central banks had been conducting a gold pool on the London gold market since 1961. They had bought and sold gold to keep the price at the monetary price, $35 an ounce. In most years since 1961, the bankers had had to buy gold in order to keep the price from falling below $35. The gold thus purchased was added to monetary reserves. But in 1967, and in the early months of 1968, the bankers had to sell very large quantities of gold to hoarders and speculators in order to keep the price on the free market from rising precipitately.

At this point, many favored a rise in the price of gold as a policy. Others believed it to be inevitable, in the face of the violent speculative gold rush. And the speculators, of course, bet it would happen.

In Washington on March 17, 1968, the active members of the gold pool agreed that no change in the dollar price of gold was necessary, and that the supply of gold in the central banks was sufficient to meet the needs of trade, in view of the prospective implementation of the Rio plan. They therefore announced that they would no longer buy or sell gold in the market, but confine the use of monetary gold stocks to transactions among the central banks, along with other reserves. In other words, they declared their freedom from the open market for gold. That market is available to industrial users of gold, and to any other private buyers who wish to purchase gold. Under the Washington agreement, and the Stockholm agreement of a larger group which affirmed its essential ideas, it should be possible to move forward rapidly to consolidate and control the world monetary system.

We have entered a new and most promising stage in the evolution of the monetary system. The essentially extraneous accident of the availability of gold should no longer limit the freedom of monetary authorities to finance economic growth and development. With the Rio plan, they should be able directly to face their responsibility for managing the world monetary system in accordance with the principles of economic stability, economic discipline, and economic need.

This conclusion does not imply that all our monetary problems will be solved when the Rio plan becomes operative. Further measures of monetary cooperation will be needed in the years ahead to establish methods for administering a system which will use several forms of reserves—gold, SDR's, and foreign-exchange balances. Prudent steps will have to be taken through cooperative action to safeguard the system during this period of transition, while adjustments are still in process, both to minimize risks and to perfect our methods of cooperation under changing circumstances.

The essential problem of the Free World economy is that of success. The volume of international trade has increased more rapidly than the capacity of the international monetary system to govern it. The need at the moment is to perfect the machinery of monetary cooperation so that monetary management can coordinate economic policy and control the process of balance-of-payments adjustment.

The pressures within the system now require a choice among three broad lines of policy: (a) flexible tariffs, advocated as a way to permit balance-of-payments adjustment; this course would lead toward protectionism and autarchy; (b) flexible exchange rates, advocated on the same ground; such policies would restrict trade and investment and would threaten anarchy in the money system; and (c) the more complete integration of the monetary systems of the chief trading nations.

Only the latter course could safeguard the gains, and the promise, of international economic cooperation during the last generation, which has opened the way toward a common market of the Free World.

Progress in the Developing World

Nineteen years have passed since President Truman first asked Americans to help build a better way of life for those people overseas who live in poverty, ignorance, sickness, and despair. Since that time, we have learned how difficult it is to help over seventy countries and one and one-half billion people achieve real economic and social progress. Despite commendable progress in countries such as Mexico, Pakistan, Venezuela, Korea, Iran, Israel, and Taiwan, in most of Asia, Africa, and Latin America the job is still not done—far from it.

But these years of success and failure have taught us a great deal about the challenges of development and its importance to our national interests. We know that prosperous democracies cannot subsist indefinitely as islands of affluence in a sea of poverty, and that on grounds both of conscience and of self-interest we must seek to end the polarization of the world into rich and poor nations. We know that it is more than coincidence that in this decade most of the conflicts threatening world peace have arisen not in Europe but in the Congo, Cuba, the Middle East, and the whole sweep of Southeast Asia. Poverty, deprivation, and hunger destroy human dignity and make progress impossible. They release primitive impulses of destruction for its own sake, and open the way to political disorders which could destroy the fabric of peace.

During the Johnson Administration, our development programs have been restructured to reflect the lessons of experience with the development process.

We have tried to view the tasks of development in the perspective of decades. We are seeking to achieve not quick dramatic returns but a cooperative international framework for global development which is soundly conceived to match the challenge. We are proceeding on the assumption that, if we succeed in maintaining peace in the world, the problem of food, education, and growth for two-thirds of humanity will hold the world's center stage for the second postwar generation, just as the Cold War held center stage for the first.

Because there are limits on the resources we can offer and the role we can play to promote development elsewhere, we have made self-help the first principle of our development assistance program. The President has been firm in reducing or suspending aid to those countries unwilling to pursue policies and programs essential to progress. As a result, many developing nations have come to realize that responsibility for progress rests chiefly with them—that only their will, their acceptance of reality, and their adoption of programs and policies capable of encouraging growth can bring modernity to their societies.

At the same time, President Johnson, at every opportunity, in every available international forum, has made clear his view that the growth of the Third World must be a collective responsibility of all the developed countries. Basing policy on the conviction that joint action is the most effective action in today's world, he has sought to develop habits of collective action by supporting international coalitions for specific tasks. This is the idea behind the Alliance for Progress in Latin America, the development of regional programs and regional banks in Asia and Africa, and our strong support for aid consortia organized by the World Bank and the International Monetary Fund. In development aid, as in peace-keeping, arms control, and international trade, our strategy has consistently been the same—a search for authentic partnerships of shared power and mutual responsibility.

With respect to the management of our own aid program, we have sought to concentrate our assistance in order to make a maximum impact in key countries and to concentrate our limited resources on those tasks which are fundamental—food, education, and health.

For the President personally the war on hunger has been an intense concern. "Next to the pursuit of peace," President Johnson said in his 1967 State of the Union Message, "the greatest challenge to the human family is the race between food supply and population increase. That race tonight is being lost."

While doing our utmost to promote agricultural revolutions abroad, our food-for-peace program has been revised so that the U.S. can grow more food to help feed the hungry in other countries. Our economic-assistance programs now give highest priority to developing countries' efforts to help increase their food production. And a central point has been established within AID for leadership and coordination of these war-on-hunger programs.

To help dampen the population explosion, the United States has provided assistance to family-planning programs in developing countries and repeatedly emphasized to foreign leaders the importance of these programs for the future of their countries.

Finally, we have emphasized that the task of development is not a task for governments alone. The need for capital and expertise in the developing world is very large—a multiple of existing or prospective aid programs, if progress is to be generated and accelerated. The knowledge, initiative, managerial experience, and capital required for development can come only from the business and professional communities of the advanced countries. Hence the Johnson Administration has been seeking, by policy and practice, to increase the flow of private resources and talents to the developing world.

One aspect of that effort was the adoption by the UNCTAD conference in 1968 of an American proposal to study the possibilities of an international treaty which could make it possible for international corporations to do business more easily in developing countries. Such a treaty would define the rights and obligations of foreign companies in signatory countries. For companies which registered under such a treaty, a presumptive right to do business would be established, subject to suitable and agreed safeguards. Such a treaty could multiply the availability to the developing countries of entrepreneurship and capital from many countries all over the world.

The pattern of foreign aid which has prevailed for twenty years has basic shortcomings, even for countries where it has helped to catalyze a positive response.

A cooperative relation between the advanced countries and the developing countries in economic planning and in the coordination of governmental policies will remain the heart of the development process for many, perhaps for most developing countries. The training of planners and administrators has been one of the most productive long-run consequences of aid programs. In recent years, many of these relationships have been organized by the World Bank or by the International Monetary Fund, as well as through bilateral cooperation between countries. In agriculture and in finance, in road building, education, public health, and many other fields, technical cooperation of this kind will have a crucial role to play for many years to come.

But improvements in governmental policies and administration are not enough to guarantee the flow of resources from abroad most developing countries require to assure economic growth and progress toward full employment. Nor is it feasible to imagine that government-to-government loans or grants can be made available on a sufficient scale to meet these needs.

A sufficient volume of capital is not of itself enough to assure success in development programs. Every developing country has learned that the efforts of government have to be supplemented by those of the private sector—both in agriculture and in industry —if the goal of development is to remain in sight. The countries which have moved ahead, and begun to provide opportunities for their people, are those which have released the energies of the market, and used the skills of private entrepreneurs to organize economic activity.

The development process is the greatest challenge to the human family, second only to the task of peace itself. It involves every country and every part of the world, for there can be no wall between the rich industrial countries, which are short of labor, and the developing nations of the Southern Hemisphere, suffering from chronic unemployment. Capital, technical skills, entrepreneurship, and assistance in the art of government will have to be attracted to the developing nations on a new scale if mankind is to avoid unimaginable tragedy.

The most melancholy statistic I know, more poignant even than the absurdity of the nuclear problem, is the fact that the rate of illiteracy is rising in the world.

CHAPTER 7

Conclusion

THESE BRIEF CHAPTERS do not pretend to encyclopedic complete-
ness as a review of recent American foreign policy. They make no
reference to many important initiatives and activities—the American role in twice preventing war between Greece and Turkey over
Cyprus, for example, the Cuban and Dominican crises, or our part
in resolving the conflict between India and Pakistan. Many significant issues are not discussed—the Alliance for Progress, the reform of the United Nations, and our developing relationships with
Japan, Canada, and the nations of Africa, to cite a few.

I have chosen rather to document and illustrate the main
themes of the argument here—that our national security can be
protected only by the establishment and acceptance of a new equilibrium of force in the world, a system of peace based on the principles of the Charter of the United Nations, a system committed
to peace, and tolerant within that framework of a wide diversity
among social systems.

The fulfillment of that goal contemplates and requires increasingly close and effective cooperation by the United States and
its allies in all the works of peace—in economic and security problems, in aid to the developing countries, in the complex politics
of achieving order and progress in a turbulent and discordant but
interdependent world. The processes for developing and enlarging

115

these patterns of cooperation, necessarily slow, are in train. It will take time before we become in fact the junior partner in regional coalitions to assure stability and development in areas of the Free World now threatened with conquest or chaos. But the policy of cooperation has achieved much in this period—enough, surely, to provide assurance that it is the soundest and most promising path to peace.

In broad perspective, American foreign policy since 1945, for all its mistakes, has been an ambitious and imaginative response to the facts of life in the new world in which we have no choice but to live. It has been conscious of change, and foresighted in seeking adaptation to change. Above all, it rests on a deeply considered perception of reality—reality tomorrow and ten years hence, the reality of history which can be invoked to guide the course of events.

But history imposes limits on the possibility of change. Societies and their ideas are tenacious, and respond slowly even to the most imperative pressures. Our own history, and the American view of the world, establish clear limits on the discretion of any President, and any Congress, in the making of foreign policy. Other countries must conduct their policies with comparable respect for their own histories, and their own outlooks.

In many ways, the tension in men's minds between the past and the present is the most important problem of foreign policy in every country. It requires the hardest kind of intellectual and moral effort to accept reality when reality requires a modification in cherished convictions, or in concepts of self built up over generations. Men are afraid of strangers and of foreigners, and many have good historical reasons for their fears. Others cling to feuds and hopes for revenge, to old grievances superseded by time.

For us, having a foreign policy at all is unnatural. Far removed from our Puritan and Calvinist past, we are reluctant to believe in the prevalence of evil, or to give the Devil his due.

The barbarities of our age—the wars themselves and the cruelties and lunacies they released—have revived the intermittent conviction of earlier centuries that war is the ultimate menace to the possibility of civilization, and that aggressive war is intolerable to human society, and therefore contrary to international law.

The pattern of political organization we have inherited from history has for centuries outraged men as anarchy—a condition in which the nations live in a constant state of war or near-war. From the beginning of time, philosophers, poets, lawyers, generals, and mystics have sought to persuade or to force men to accept world governments that seemed to them more rational. Thus far, they have failed. Bitter and intractable aspects of our social experience have defeated all man's yearning efforts to banish war, and fulfill his dreams of progressive peace.

The force of that fact in our history must be acknowledged, not as an argument against idealism, but as the inescapable starting point for study. It is easy to escape the burden of reality in the pleasure of constructing perfect models. And the making of Utopias has often had a profound and on the whole a beneficent long-term effect on the behavior of men. But the risk of war in this generation is urgent and real. It must be dealt with in terms of immediacies or there may be no significant long-term future for which to plan. It is not difficult to imagine a more sensible world constitution than the one we have inherited. But we can't stop the world and get off until some such plan is adopted. We cannot evade the ordeal of seeking to achieve peace within the present system because the world is badly organized. The world is indeed badly organized, but that fact is not immediately relevant to the problem of peace.

If, then, we take the world as it is, we must start with the proposition of the older diplomacy, which is the heart of the United Nations Charter, namely, that the Great Powers have special duties in conducting the politics of the society of nations. Like most duties in law and in life, the responsibilities of the Great Powers arise out of circumstance. They are the policemen of the world political system because they alone have the capacity to discharge that function. And if they fail, as they have so often

117

failed in this century, the consequences may be not merely catastrophic but seemingly permanent as well, for themselves and for everyone else. In order to have any hope of fulfilling their task as Great Powers effectively, they should act not only with prudence, patience, and mutual restraint, but with a sense of shared membership in a single human community as well.

Since World War II, the United States had to take on much of the burden of maintaining a world equilibrium. Given the postwar weakness of France and Britain, Europe and then Asia and the Middle East had no choice but to seek American protection. And, if our own national interests were to be secured, we had no real choice but to undertake the burden. At the time, we were the only nation capable of resisting aggression. It therefore became our obligation to do so. We accepted the charge, in a series of steps starting in Iran and Turkey, and including Greece, Yugoslavia, Berlin, and then Korea and Vietnam. The United States became in effect the surrogate for the entire Free World, to whom the responsibilities of Great Powership were delegated for a time.

Our course, embodied in the arrangements for the conduct of NATO and for protecting South Korea and South Vietnam, rests on the tradition of concerted Great Power action to prevent or to confine war. That tradition has been developing, through a series of hopeful trials and tragic errors, at least since 1812. In the last century, a concert of Great Powers managed to preserve a tolerably secure system that prevented the possibility of major successful aggression. On that political base of balanced power, there grew up a great network of international law, practice, and institutions that made it possible to imagine a system of world law as secure as that within a single civilized nation.

This evolutionary process was interrupted by World War I. The old balance could no longer contain the aggressive impulses of Germany. After thirty years of tension and struggle, the entire network of world order fell to the ground. We have lived through a half century of retreat in the quest for rationality in world politics.

Since World War II, we have been seeking to building the foundations for a new system. We have used American power to shield the resurgence of old nations and the birth pangs of new. We have sought to establish several regional concerts of powers as the political base for an increasing rule of law in the world. In the nature of our political ethos the United States cannot conduct an imperial foreign policy. But we can shed our isolationist past and become partners in collective efforts to secure a progressive and stable peace. For twenty years we have sought to build coalitions which could make the precedents of restraint implicit in the Truman Doctrine into a common law of international behavior.

Thus far, neither the Soviet Union nor Communist China has fully accepted this prudent idea as the basis for a policy of coexistence. On the other hand, neither one has declared full war against it. They have sought to evade the logic of the rule without rejecting it, or its benefits. In 1948, 1953, 1956, and again in 1968, the Soviet Union brutally put down movements of national freedom in Eastern Europe, confident that we would not threaten nuclear warfare to stop her. But thus far the Soviet Union has refused to accept the corollary. She has continued to encourage processes of conquest in Asia, the Middle East, and in Africa, and has not stopped Castro's activities in Latin America.

While American patience has been great, it cannot be expected indefinitely to respect the rule of the Truman Doctrine without reciprocity. There can be no peace until the Soviet Union and Communist China genuinely accept the logic of coexistence.

The Truman Doctrine, after all, is not an end but a means to an end. It represents only the idea of a minimal degree of order in the world, which could evolve toward a condition of true peace. The rules against aggression in the United Nations Charter are universal in character. They are not confined to the Free World. The United States has repeatedly pointed out that the territorial integrity and political independence of Czechoslovakia and Hungary are as much entitled to international protection as those of

119

Korea and Israel. As President Kennedy recalled in 1961, the Yalta Agreement and the Potsdam Agreement provided for a free choice for the people of Eastern Europe. "We believe," he remarked, "that if the Soviet Union will permit the people of the world to live as they wish to live, relations between the Soviet Union and the United States will then be satisfactory, and our two peoples, which now live in danger, will be able to live in peace."

Thus far, we have said, the national interests of the United States and its allies could tolerate a modus vivendi based on the idea of the Truman Doctrine. The goal of that modus vivendi, and the condition for its survival, is that it become something more—a process through which tensions could be reduced and the fear of aggression eliminated in the relations among states.

For the United States and its allies, there is no real alternative to the pursuit of détente, the only foreign policy which offers mankind the hope of peace. The pursuit of détente cannot, and should not, rest on illusion about the nature of Soviet or Chinese policy. However prudent and restrained, it should be more than a policy of turning the other cheek. But it can never lose sight of its basic aim, however severe the temptation.

Those who see the history of the postwar years only as a history of cold war, of containment, and of economic and social development in the Free World behind the shield of American power miss the point. The United States has never given up the search, with its allies, for an understanding with the Soviet Union and with Communist China. The history of this period is not only one of tracing the consequences of Soviet and Chinese actions clanging shut many gates to collaboration, it is a history also of persistent American efforts to keep them open.

There are tides in the process of seeking an understanding with the Communist states. In 1968, the Western allies took two major steps which they had reason to hope might persuade the Soviet Union to allow political relations between East and West to improve. NATO proposed the joint examination of plans for a reduction of forces and for agreements of arms limitation in Central Europe. Such negotiations could lead to a new system of European security, far less tense and burdensome than the massive confrontation of rival armies which has been the rule in Europe for twenty years. In such discussions, President Johnson has said, "no topic would be barred." Secondly, the West joined the Soviet Union in sponsoring the Non-Proliferation Treaty—an agreement which could only become genuinely effective in a climate of peaceful coexistence.

The Soviet invasion and occupation of Czechoslovakia in August, 1968, attacked the premise of these efforts. The Soviet Union took the view that a movement toward ordinary human liberty in Czechoslovakia threatened the security of the Soviet Union and its allies in Eastern Europe. For the moment, it set itself completely against the policy of détente—against more relaxed human contacts of many kinds; against trade and tourism between Eastern and Western Europe; against an atmosphere of more freedom in the dialogue of scholars, students, and other citizens from both sides of the ideological boundary.

This turn of Soviet policy represents profound fear—a fear of the future and of the people. It remains to be seen how it will affect Soviet activities in other areas relevant to the possibility of détente—Vietnam and Korea, the Middle East, and Cuba.

The NATO proposals for arms limitation understandings offered the Soviet Union a more secure and constructive approach to the problem of its safety in a world of change. The police methods of Stalin can doubtless work for a time in repressing the peoples of Eastern Europe and the Soviet Union, as they have worked before. But such methods lead in turn to violent answers, and more extreme forms of opposition than might otherwise have appeared.

Meanwhile, the United States and its allies have to respond to the impact of these events on their own security. Soviet troops have moved forward in large numbers from the Soviet Union to Poland, East Germany, and Czechoslovakia. Both this fact, and the demonstration of Soviet willingness to use force, affect the mission of NATO in defending Western Europe and the Mediterranean.

The deterrent power of NATO and of the Sixth Fleet should suffice for the moment to protect allied interests in Western Europe and the Mediterranean. But the direct use of force by the Soviet Union for the first time in twelve years may have more fundamental implications. What light does this decision cast on the intentions of the rulers of the Soviet Union, and on their willingness to use force elsewhere?

The only prudent response of the allies must be to accelerate the improvement in their methods of cooperation. It would be idle to expect significant progress toward a regime of peaceful coexistence for some time. The invasion of Czechoslovakia has made the world political system more precarious and less stable than before.

The achievement of closer concert in our alliances, both in Europe and in Asia, should therefore remain the first principle of our political strategy. Such a development could result in a more equitable sharing of the burdens of responsibility than now prevails. It should thus establish a base for American action less vulnerable to isolationist attack at home than is the case at the present time. In such a posture, the allies could renew their request for conciliation with the Soviet Union and with Communist China on the basis of reciprocal policies intended to reduce tensions.

But the use of force in Eastern Europe, as President Johnson has said, "generates fears and stimulates passions whose consequences no man can predict or control." The primary mission of NATO was, and is, to defend the allies, not to enforce the Potsdam and Yalta agreements calling for free elections in Germany and in Eastern Europe. But the expectations which determined the Western policy of restraint in the early postwar years when the Soviet Union undertook to divide Europe and to dominate the countries of Eastern Europe might not survive another period of Stalinism.

The heart of the security problem, for the United States and for the whole Free World, is summed up in a single question: Will the United States continue to elect Presidents who have the courage and sense of duty to do what President Truman did in Korea, Berlin, Greece, Turkey, and Iran; what President Kennedy was ready to do in Cuba; and what President Johnson did in the Middle East and Vietnam? Until the American mind finally overcomes its isolationist past, such actions by an American President can only hurt him at home. President Truman and President Johnson were destroyed politically by Korea and Vietnam. Those who imagine that an American President can ever prefer war, or resist a fair opportunity to make peace, ignore this basic political reality. An American President is always tempted to accept feeble and unstable compromises, such as those which were made for Indochina in 1954 and 1955, and for the Middle East in 1956 and 1957. Those settlements failed to protect the security interests of the United States; they guaranteed future trouble. But so long as large segments of American opinion resist the reality of the twentieth century, any American President will be under severe pressure to prefer them.

The best—the only—answer to this disease of the American will is allied unity and a full sharing of allied responsibility. The course of unity is the course of prudence for our allies as it is for us. For reasons deep in our history, American opinion will accept sharing collective responsibility just as strongly as it rebels against the lonely burdens we have had to bear since 1945. The time has passed when those who depend upon American protection can afford the position of "having one's cake and eating it too," which was so irresponsibly enjoyed during the nineteenth century, and the first part of this one as well.

The peace can no longer be kept by tacit understandings between the Soviet Union and the United States. In our polycentric world, it is increasingly difficult for the two Great Powers to contain local turbulence and prevent it from threatening the general peace. The world is becoming more unstable. And instability is a primary cause of war. On this lunatic planet, war can come, even in the absence of a Napoleon or a Hitler, when one or more of the players gets tired or desperate, when he feels a strong current setting in, a current in which he feels he might drown unless he strikes out.

If peace is to be achieved—indeed, if war is to be avoided—there is no alternative to Soviet and Chinese acceptance of the idea of peaceful coexistence as part of the common law of international life. Such a step would make the system of world politics less precarious than it is. But it could not be expected to usher in a new dawn of perfect harmony. The world will produce new problems even if the ideological element in modern politics should completely disappear. Human vitality and the power of evil will continue to challenge the best-constructed schemes of order.

For five years, a debate has raged about our policy in Vietnam. That, at least, has been its nominal subject matter. The real theme of the debate has been whether the United States should have a foreign policy, and what role force should play in carrying it out—whether our interests are world-wide or confined to the small circle of rich, industrial countries; whether we can defend our national interests without exertion, and without sacrifice.

In the course of this debate some distinguished and high-minded leaders have promised the American people painless and costless safety—security without tears, and the freedom to ignore the outside world and devote all their energies to the solution of our social problems at home.

It is the thesis of this book that such soft promises are illusory. There is a general shortage of campaign orators willing to promise nothing but blood, sweat, and tears.

There is no way for the United States to escape responsible involvement in the struggle to assure world peace and world progress. Our strength is indispensable to the possibility of success.

And we cannot immunize ourselves against the consequences of failure.

The prospects for peace deny us the luxury of escape or of facile optimism. There is no reason either for despair. The United States and its allies have more than enough power and wealth to carry through in the effort to achieve equilibrium in the world, if they do not lose their nerve or their will.

We cannot expect to protect our national interests in the world of the late twentieth century if our minds are still dominated by the ideas of the nineteenth century. Twenty-three years after the end of the Second World War, we should understand the forces which shape the world environment. And, most especially, we should at last have come to terms with the role of power in international society.

Wisdom, patience, and luck can confine power, and subject its use to the control of law. But they cannot exorcise it or deny its role in the quest for peace. Of all the ideas which cloud our perception of reality, perhaps the most deceptive is the hardy Utopianism which has come down to us from our isolated and protected experience during the nineteenth century. It is an attractive creed, for all its naïveté, the source of much that is good in American attitudes and American policy. What we must guard against is the illusion that law can prevail without force, either within societies or in the society of nations.

We learned early in our national experience that the frontier was unlikely to be a paradise without a marshal and the United States cavalry. The same principles apply to the relations among nations. Law cannot be imposed—in free societies, at least—by force alone. And even in societies of consent law must be sustained by public force backing the general will. In international society, law is inconceivable without the rational and agreed control of force.

Index

Africa
  aid to developing nations in, 110, 111
  in nineteenth century, 25
AID, 112
Alexander I, Emperor of Russia, 19, 27
Algeria, 77, 80
Alliance for Progress in Latin America, 111
Aqaba, Gulf of, 78, 79
Arab states, 74–75, 77
  Israel opposed by, 75–77
  Soviet arms shipments to, 76
  War with Israel, 75, 77–82
  Six-Day War, 73, 80
Asia, Southeast, see Southeast Asia
Atlantic Alliance, see NATO
Atomic weapons, see Nuclear weapons
Australia, 72
Austrian Empire, 28, 31

Balance of payments, 103–107
Balance of power, 10, 26, 38
  United States and, 40
Balfour Declaration, 75
Ball, George W., 3
Bao Dai, 60

Baruch Plan for international control of nuclear energy, 37
Belgium, decolonization, 41
Benda, Julien, Trahison des Clercs, 16
Bentham, Jeremy, 26
Berlin, 45, 118
  blockade, 13, 15, 53
Bourguiba, President of Tunisia, quoted, 68–69
Bretton Woods agreements, 102
Britain, see Great Britain
Brogan, D. W., quoted, 21–22
Burma, 66
Byron, George Gordon, Lord, 28

Cambodia, 60
Canada, 96, 107
Castlereagh, Robert Stewart, Viscount, 19, 27–29
Castro, Fidel, 11, 45, 119
China
  Japanese aggression in, 33
  in Security Council, 14
China, Communist, 15, 25, 52, 53, 62, 119, 120, 122, 124
  recognition of, 14, 90
  Soviet alliance with, 37
  in United Nations, vote on, 90

China, Communist (*Cont.*)
United States policy on, 89–90
in Vietnam War, 14, 66–67
China, Republic of, 61, 72
Churchill, Sir Winston, 35
Cicero, xvi
Cobden, Richard, 26
Cold War, responsibility for, xiv–xv
Collective security in United Nations Charter, 6–8
Collective unconscious, 37, 38
Colonies, *see* Decolonization
Communist nations
limited aggression by, 12–13, 15, 47, 48
United States attitude toward, 44–45
Communists
in developing countries, 53
in Europe, 34
power of, 41
Congress of Vienna, 7, 18, 19, 22–24, 27–28
Crimean War, 31
Cuba, missile crisis, 3, 45, 54
Czechoslovakia, 119
Soviet invasion of, 45, 89, 121, 122

Declaration of Independence, 20
Decolonization, 41, 44, 51
in Middle East, 77
Democracy, 20
Developing nations, 41, 62, 102
aid to, 51–52, 110–114
Communists in, 53

EFTA, 103, 107
Egypt in Israeli-Arab war, 77–78, 80
1848, revolutions of, xvii, 22, 31
Eilat, 78
Eisenhower, Dwight D., 67
Southeast Asia policy, 61, 63, 64

England, *see* Great Britain
Europe
in nineteenth century, 22–23, 25–26
postwar reconstruction programs, 102
in twentieth century, 34–35, 40
1960s, 52, 92–93
United States cooperation with, 91–101
Europe of the Six, 102

Fairbank, John, 25
Foreign aid, *see* Developing nations
Foreign policy, *see* United States
Formosa, *see* Taiwan
Fowler, Henry H., 105
France
American and British leadership protested by, 33–34
decolonization, 41
Geneva agreements on Indochina, 60
Germany, cooperation with, 93–95
NATO military forces, withdrawal from, 98
Quadruple Alliance and, 28–29
radical movements in, 21–22
in Security Council, 13–14
strikes in, 13, 107–108
Franco-Prussian War, 31
French Revolution, 18–21, 26, 30

GATT, 102, 103, 107
Gaza Strip, 77–78
Genêt, Edmond (Citizen), 30
Geneva Accords on Southeast Asia, 60–61, 67, 70
Germany, 94–95, 118
France, cooperation with, 93–95
nationalism, 31, 32
in NATO agreements, 98–100
Germany, East, 45

Gibbon, Edward, 32
Great Britain
  decolonization, 41
  devaluation of pound, 106
  in European community, 95
  Israel established by, 75
  in Israeli-Arab war, 79
  in NATO agreement, 98
  nuclear weapons treaty signed, 88
  Parliament, functions of, 5–6
  Quadruple Alliance, 28–29
  in Security Council, 13–14
  United States relations with, 33
Great Powers
  aggression by, 10–11
  in nineteenth century, 22, 28, 30
  peace-keeping diplomacy, 10
  in Security Council, 7–9, 13–14, 117–118
Greece, 42, 118
  civil war, 13, 14

Hanoi, see Vietnam, North
Harding, Warren G., 51
Hinsley, F. H., quoted, 23–24
Hitler, Adolf, 32, 39, 54
Ho Chi Minh, 60, 71
Hughes, Charles Evans, 32–33
Hungary, 45, 119

Illiteracy, increase of, 114
India, 62, 63
  British influence in, 25
  war with Pakistan, 48,
Indochina, see Southeast Asia
Indonesia, 62, 63, 72
INTELSAT, 92
International law
  force and, 11
  principles of, 1–3, 15–16
International Monetary Fund, 103, 111, 113
  Special Drawing Rights Plan, 105, 106, 109
Iran, 13, 42, 45, 62, 75, 110, 118

Iraq, 77, 80
Isolationism, 33, 34, 38, 39, 51, 54–56, 97
Israel, 62, 110, 120
  Arab opposition to, 75–77
  founding of, 75
  Soviet policy on, 76
  United States attitude toward, 75
  war with Arab states, 75, 77–82
    Six-Day War, 73, 80
Italy
  strikes in, 13
  unification of, 31

Japan, 72, 92, 102
  China attacked by, 33
  European methods adapted to, 24
  United States relations with, 49, 51, 52, 61, 91
  in world affairs, 96, 98, 107
Jarring, Ambassador, 82
Jefferson, Thomas, 30
Jerusalem, protection of, 81
Johnson, Lyndon B., 51, 52, 54, 55, 58, 95, 106, 121
  on Communist China, 89–90
  developing nations, aid to, 111
  foreign policy, 56–57
  in Israeli-Arab war, 78–81
  Middle East policy, 78–83
  in monetary crisis, 107
  on NATO, 90–91, 97, 99–100
  quoted, 64–65, 78, 83, 86, 89–90, 112, 122
  Soviet Union policy, 86, 88
  Vietnam policy, 59, 63, 64, 67, 69–72
  withdrawal from election, 72
Johnson Administration, 49, 53, 59, 101, 110, 112
Jordan in Israeli-Arab war, 77, 80
Jung, Carl Gustav, collective unconscious, 37

Kant, Immanuel, 26
Kennedy, John F., 43, 68, 95, 120
  tariff negotiations (Kennedy Round), 98, 102, 106, 107
  Vietnam policy, 63, 67
Kissinger, Henry A., quoted, 28–29
Korea, 61, 62, 72, 110, 118, 120
Korean War, 13, 15, 45, 47, 54, 56
  United Nations in, 3, 7–8
Kosygin, Alexi, 70
Kuwait, 80

Laos, 13, 60, 66, 67
Latin America, aid to, 110, 111, 114
Law, international, see International law
League of Nations, 6, 32
  Covenant, 10
  United States and, 33, 55, 56
Lenin, Nikolai, 18

McCarthy, Senator Joseph, 56
Malaysia, 62, 63, 72
Mao Tse-tung, Cultural Revolution, 19
Marshall Plan, 37, 42, 54, 56, 93, 102
Metternich, Klemens von, 19, 27–28
Mexico, 110
Middle East, 53, 54, 73–84
  Soviet policy on, 49, 74–76
  United States policy on, 59, 73–74, 78–84, 87
Mill, James, 26
Moheiddin, Zachariah, 79
Monetary policy, 98, 102–110
  balance of payments, 103–107
  European surplus, 107–108
  gold reserve, 105, 108–109
Monnet, Jean, quoted, xiii
Montaigne, Michel Eyquem de, 17

Montesquieu, Charles de Secondat, Baron de, xvi
Muslims, 74
  see also Arab states

Namier, Lewis B., quoted, 31
Napoleon, 23, 26
Nasser, Gamal Abdel, 45
  in Israeli-Arab war, 77, 78, 80
Nationalism, 20, 31–32
NATO, 42, 45, 49, 51, 87, 90–101
  France withdraws from, 98
  military forces, 98, 100–101, 122
  political responsibilities, 98, 99
  reorganization, 97–99
  Soviet Union and, 100–101, 120, 121
Near East, see Middle East
Nehru, Jawaharlal, quoted, 12
Netherlands, decolonization, 41
New Zealand, 72.
Nkrumah, Kwame, 45
Nobel, Alfred, 17
North Atlantic Alliance, see NATO
North Atlantic Council, 88, 99
Nuclear energy, Baruch Plan for international control of, 37
Nuclear weapons, 96.
  NATO consultations on, 98
  treaty on, 87–88, 98, 120–121
  United States monopoly of, 45

OECD, 93, 103, 107
Ortega y Gasset, José, 20

Pakistan, 62, 110
  war with India, 48,
Peace
  problem of, xiii–xviii, 49
  world, as ideal, 26–27
Peaceful coexistence, 49, 52, 54, 119, 124
Philippines, 72

Point Four program, 102

Potsdam Agreement, 42, 43, 120, 122

Pound, Roscoe, x–xi

Quadruple Alliance, 28–29

Rio de Janeiro monetary agreement, 98, 106, 108, 109

Roosevelt, Franklin Delano, 33

Rousseau, Jean Jacques, 26, 32

Rusk, Dean, xv

Russia, see Soviet Union

Russian Empire, 28, 46

Russian Revolution, 32, 34, 46, 47

Saigon, see Vietnam, South

Satellite communications, 88, 92, 98

Saudi Arabia, 75

SEATO Treaty, 61, 63–67

Sharm-al-Sheikh, 78

Shelley, Percy Bysshe, 28

Sinai peninsula, 77, 78

Southeast Asia, 53, 59–60
   Geneva agreements on, 60–61
   SEATO Treaty, 61, 63–67
   United States policy on, 61–62, 72

Soviet Union
   Communist China, alliance with, 37
   Cuban missile crisis, 3, 45, 54
   Czechoslovakia invaded, 45, 89, 121, 122
   Israel, policy on, 76
   loans offered to, 102
   Middle East policy, 49, 74–76
   military forces in Europe, 100, 121
   NATO and, 100–101, 121
   nuclear weapons treaty, 87–88, 120
   peaceful coexistence, 49, 52, 54, 119, 124
   in Security Council, 13, 37
   United States relations with, 15, 36–37, 45–48, 53, 86–89, 119, 120–121
     cooperation, possibility of, 86–88
   in Vietnam War, 14, 49, 66–67, 69–70
   as world power, 13, 34–35
   Yalta and Potsdam agreements broken, 42

Space program
   satellites, 88, 92, 98
   Treaty on the Peaceful Use of Outer Space, 88–89

Stalin, Joseph, 45

Stendhal, The Charterhouse of Parma, 23

Stimson, Henry L., 32–33

Suez Canal, Egyptian control of, 78

Suez crisis, 46, 48, 77

Sukarno, Achmed, 45

Syria, 75, 77
   in Israeli-Arab war, 77, 80

Taiwan, 62, 110

Tariff negotiations, 98, 102, 106, 107

Thailand, 62, 66, 72

Tiran, Strait of, 78, 79

Tolstoy, Leo, Anna Karenina, 46

Tonkin Gulf, 63

Treaty on the Peaceful Use of Outer Space, 88–89

Treaty of Westphalia, 18

Truman, Harry S., 40, 43, 54, 58, 110
   quoted, 42

Truman Doctrine, 13, 16–17, 42–45, 49, 56, 119, 120
   threats to, 52, 53
   Vietnam War and, 67, 68, 70, 72

Tunisia, 75

Turkey, 13, 42, 75, 118

UNCTAD, 112
United Arab Republic, see Arab states; Egypt; other countries
United Nations
  attitudes toward, 3–4, 41
  Communist China, admission of, 90
  in Israeli-Arab war, 77, 79, 80, 82
  in Korean War, 3, 7–8
  powers of, 4–9
  Security Council
    aggression by members of, 14
    Great Powers in, 7–9, 13–14
    in Israeli-Arab war, 77, 79, 80, 82
    responsibility of, 7
    Soviet Union veto, 37
United Nations Charter, xvii, 10, 15, 16, 57, 66, 115, 119
  collective security in, 6–8
  Great Powers in, 13, 117–118
  on wars, legal and illegal, 3
United States
  Britain, relations with, 33
  and Communist nations, 44–45
  Cuban missile crisis, 3, 45, 54
  economic policy, 101–103
  financial crisis, 106
  force used by, 11
  foreign policy, 44, 49, 51–52, 55–59, 85–87, 101–102, 115–120
    in Europe, 91–101
    on Middle East, see Middle East
    social progress and, 55–56
    on Vietnam, see Vietnam
  idealism versus power politics, 4–5, 39
  isolationism, see Isolationism
  Japan, relations with, 49, 51, 52, 61, 91
  and League of Nations, 33, 55, 56

monetary policy, 98, 102–110
  in NATO agreement, 98
  peace-keeping responsibility, 11–15, 44
  race problems, 11
  revolutionary tradition, 44–45
  in Security Council, 13
  Soviet Union, relations with, 15, 36–37, 45–48, 53, 86–89, 120–121
    cooperation, possibility of, 86–88
  tax legislation, 106
  in world politics, 36–38, 40–42
  as world power, 13, 34–35
Universities, 96
Utopianism, 39, 125

Vattel, Emmerich von, 32
Venezuela, 110
Vietminh, Geneva agreements on, 60
Vietnam
  Communist aggression in, 14, 47
  Geneva agreements on, 60–61
  unification of, 60–61
  United States policy on, 59–73, 87, 118
Vietnam, North, 60–62
  bombing of, 64, 70–72
  Soviet aid to, 49, 67
  United States negotiations with, 70–72
  in war, 62–63, 65
Vietnam, South, 60–62
  elections in, 72
  United States commitment in, 65–69
  in war, 62–63, 65
Vietnam War, 13–15, 48, 56, 63–65, 70–71
  allied forces in, 72
  Communist China in, 14, 66–67
  Congress resolution on, 63–64

Vietnam War (Cont.)
  guerrilla forces, 62–63
  peace talks, 72
  public opinion against, 54–56, 72–73
  Soviet Union in, 14, 49, 66–67, 69–70
  United States participation authorized, 63–64

Wallace, Henry, 56
War as lawful act, 2–3
Washington, George, Farewell Address, 38
William II, Emperor of Germany, 23, 32

Wilson, Harold, 70
Wilson, Woodrow, 51, 55, 97
  quoted, 5–6
Wordsworth, William, 28
World Bank, 103, 111, 113
World government, hope for, 5, 26, 27, 32
World War I, 32, 39, 54, 118
World War II, 54, 56
  conditions leading to, 34–35, 40
  end of, 36

Yalta Agreement, 42, 43, 120, 122
Yemen, 77
Yugoslavia, 118

COLOPHON BOOKS ON POLITICAL SCIENCE

William Benton	THE VOICE OF LATIN AMERICA, rev. ed. CN 16
Wilfred E. Binkley	THE MAN IN THE WHITE HOUSE: His Powers and Duties. CN 46
Alastair Buchan	WAR IN MODERN SOCIETY. CN 125
Joseph S. Clark	CONGRESS: The Sapless Branch. CN 58
Richard Crossman, Ed.	THE GOD THAT FAILED. CN 26
Louis Fischer	MEN AND POLITICS: Europe Between the Two World Wars. CN 96
Louis Fischer	THE LIFE OF LENIN. CN 69
Charles Frankel	THE DEMOCRATIC PROSPECT. CN 29
Richard Grunberger	GERMANY: 1918-1945. CN 86
Samuel Lubell	THE FUTURE OF AMERICAN POLITICS, 3rd rev. ed. CN 74
Samuel Lubell	WHITE AND BLACK: Test of a Nation, 2nd rev. ed. CN 75
Roscoe C. Martin	GRASS ROOTS: Rural Democracy in America. CN 68
Anthony Sampson	ANATOMY OF BRITAIN TODAY. CN 76
Renzo Sereno	THE RULERS. CN 126
Robert Shaplen	THE LOST REVOLUTION: The United States in Vietnam, 1946-1966, rev. ed. CN 92
Kalman H. Silvert	THE CONFLICT SOCIETY: Reaction and Revolution in Latin America. CN 130*
Edmund Stillman and William Pfaff	THE NEW POLITICS: America and the End of the Postwar World. CN 5
Edmund Stillman and William Pfaff	THE POLITICS OF HYSTERIA: The Sources of Twentieth Century Conflict. CN 49
Robert Strausz-Hupé, et al	PROTRACTED CONFLICT: A Study of Communist Strategy. CN 11
Charles Vereker	THE DEVELOPMENT OF POLITICAL THEORY. CN 73

*In Preparation

COLOPHON BOOKS ON POLITICAL SCIENCE

William Benton   THE VOICE OF LATIN AMERICA, rev. ed. cn 19

Wilfred E. Binkley   THE MAN IN THE WHITE HOUSE:
His Powers and Duties, cn 46

Alastair Buchan   WAR IN MODERN SOCIETY, cn 24

Joseph S. Clark   CONGRESS: The Sapless Branch, cn 58

Richard Crossman, Ed.   THE GOD THAT FAILED, cn 30

Louis Fischer   MEN AND POLITICS:
Europe Between the Two World Wars, cn 99

THE LIFE OF LENIN, cn 69

Charles Frankel   THE DEMOCRATIC PROSPECT, cn 23

Richard Chamberlin   GERMANY 1918-1945 cn 60

Samuel Lubell   THE FUTURE OF AMERICAN POLITICS,
3rd rev. ed. cn 72

Samuel Lubell   WHITE AND BLACK: Test of a Nation,
2nd rev. ed. cn 75

Roscoe C. Martin   GRASSROOTS:
Rural Democracy in America, cn 63

Anthony Sampson   ANATOMY OF BRITAIN TODAY, cn 9

Renzo Sereno   THE RULERS, cn 106

Robert Sherrill   THE LOST PRIORITY: The United States in
Vietnam 1946-1966, cn 68, cn 92

Kalman H. Silvert   THE CONFLICT SOCIETY: Reaction and
Revolution in Latin America cn 120*

Edmund Stillman and
William Pfaff   THE NEW POLITICS: America and the End of the
Postwar World

Edmund Stillman and
William Pfaff   THE POLITICS OF HYSTERIA: The Sources of
Twentieth-Century Conflict cn 79

Robert Strausz-Hupé et al   PROTRACTED CONFLICT: A Study of
Communist Strategy cn 21

Charles Vereker   THE DEVELOPMENT OF POLITICAL THEORY
cn 93

*In Preparation